# A Tribe of Women

Janet —
You are so
special to me!
So glad you've in
my life. Let's DO
Mexico!

Blessings Always —

Kathleen
Sweeney

# A Tribe of Women

## A Memoir

### Kathleen Sweeney

First Printing: June 2020

ISBN 978-1-7352317-1-6 ebook

ISBN 978-1-7352317-2-3 paperback

# Dedication

This is dedicated to all the women
who have been, who are, and who will be.
This is your story, as much as it is mine.
May you all step into your own image and
likeness,

# TABLE OF CONTENTS

# The Guide Speaks

It is called The Summons and it comes in many different ways. For some it's herald is an urge so strong it cannot be overcome; for others it is a simmering familiarity of a long-repressed memory. Still for others, it comes through dreams, soul-rousing dreams, as inexplicable as they are intimate. The Summons has called forth to every woman throughout time, for it is inherent within the cellular structure of us all. It beckons through our Mother Tongue, a language that courses through our bodies, our hearts, our instincts; and when heeded inspires both our minds and our actions. It has a purpose, that purpose being our ability to protect and enhance the great Circle of All Life; adhere to it and it will strengthen the wisdom women carry, the force we yield. If heard, yet left unheeded, it can fester inside the belly of our souls, twisting the force and grace we carry into self-deceit and weakness, unraveling the balance of all that is. You've seen it happen; you've watched humanity become cold, cruel, greedy; empty of compassion. This is not human nature–it is a result! The result of what you call "the fall in the Garden of Eden." Make no mistake, my sisters, you have been deceived. Eve's story was a parable and a warning–but do you truly see how it has played out?

# Chapter 1–The Awakening

It was on the Hopi reservation that I first began to sense it, then in the Yucatan it began to fill me; in Hawaii I could feel it and recognize it, but it was on the ocean that I truly began to hear it and was finally able to give it a name–our Mother Tongue–a language that has been obscured and diminished for over 2,000 years. A language that was given to women through our bond with Earth and the Mother Goddess. The Divine Feminine. A force without which has led to imbalance, for The Divine Feminine has been suppressed for thousands of years.

My name is Kathleen, a woman well into her crone years, which has probably given me the courage to finally write my story-I have something I want to say! My journey has sparked within me the desire to become a born-again Pagan. A Pagan aligned with the Wise Women of Old. I claim this alignment simply because it feels so right, so in line with my heart and soul.

There cannot be too few of us who do not recognize the pain that is swarming and crippling our planet and all those who live upon her. We all know something is wrong and has been wrong for far too long. We are faced with an insulated, warring, hierarchical leadership supporting an economic and politically dominant class structure; a self-centered, polarized people so out of balance and out of touch with our planet that even the ability to intuit destruction has been lost.

But polarization cannot occur unless there is a severe imbalance and it is this imbalance I would like to address. How did it happen? Why does it continue with no thought or recognition of it's being a disease? Phrases like 'it's always been this way, it will never change' are simply untrue; repeated only by those heavily invested in its perpetuity. I do not believe we are too stupid to change, to look past this dogma, but we do have to look into our most secret and sometimes scary places for an answer. I have something to ask you:

What if you had the courage to roll back the corner stone of your most cherished and basic belief; what if you found that the very foundation it was based on was, in fact, out of balance? What if that most cherished and basic belief was the Spiritual truth you never before would have questioned, never would have dared to challenge? What if you found that it was so out of balance that anything built upon it was destined to become polarized, destined to bring an economic, social hierarchical duality and nothing else could possibly have occurred?

How would life had been different if we had been Spiritually empowered by both a Father God and a Mother Goddess? What if, rather than just one single deity owning all spiritual truth, we actually had a Spiritual Family—Mother, Father, Sister, Brother, Grandmother, Grandfathers? What if that difference included, from the very beginning, a Spiritual and Holistic education empowering all to view life not through dualism or hierarchy but as a great circle which honored all equally? What if the moral teachings were not about virginity and acquiescence, but the responsibility to protect earth and all creatures on it; and the moral responsibility to see to the health and welfare of all living on Earth? What if that Mother Goddess is still alive? Still calling? What if we

3

women were, albeit unwittingly, far more responsible for this imbalance than we have ever thought? Simply because we no longer heed Her call? Ouch!

So many 'what ifs', but wait, there is a hope. For within each and every woman there is a bond of such unique power with Mother Earth and The Goddess that it would shock you! And with it a responsibility to speak for every living creature within the Circle of Life. My journey has been all about waking up to that power, waking up to that responsibility. I'd like to share with you all the experiences I've had that have led me to roll back the cornerstone of my own imbalanced beliefs.

It is not my intention to replace God with Goddess, or anything else for that matter. For to choose yet another hierarchical expression of Spirituality–be it God or Goddess–would be to undermine the balance we need so desperately. It is quite possible that the demand for supremacy of one Deity over another may very well have been the primal suicide of everything that is good and sacred in humanity.

This book, as was my journey, is a challenge to every woman to take a really good look at what we have forgotten; at our part, even unknowingly, in prolonging this unbalanced human effect upon our world and every creature living with us. My journey, was a quest to awaken the wisdom of the Goddess that lies within me and hopefully pass it on to each and every woman who reads this. How that wisdom will manifest in you, I am not sure, for each of us is an individual, and it will manifest for you in your own unique way. We are Her Ambassadors, and maybe soon we will be Her Midwife, restoring health and balance to every aspect of our lives. We are connected to Earth and the Goddess as sisters, grandmothers, daughters, as a Tribe. It's time to remember how to listen, how to trust that call and our own innate wisdom; it's time to heed that plaintive call of our Mother Earth and the Goddess; it's time to see through the eyes of a woman, stand up and face the Moon!

# Chapter 2-The Beginning

My path took me from a catholic childhood in Seattle, to a tiny restaurant in Flagstaff, Arizona, the Hopi Mesas, a deserted beach in San Bernardino and finally a sailing journey, first with my husband then solo, across the vast amazing Oceans. People often ask what it was like to sail these incredible waters of ours and I never know quite how to answer that. For me, it was what I can only imagine a long-extended Vision Quest would feel like; or a total immersion into the world and language of The Archetypal Feminine. For within those archetypal feminine waters, unplugged from every sensory input of our lives, I emerged from an upside-down world–the one I had been living in–to a world right side up again. But first, we should start at the beginning.

I began this lifetime's journey as the second child, first girl in a Catholic family of 10 children. I was happy, curious and had an uncanny, natural sense of the mystical. The ghostly fingers of that mystical sense began to touch me early in life, with those rare and inexpiable occurrences that both thrill yet scare the pants off you; things like hitting an invisible wall that wouldn't let me out of my bedroom, lights floating around my bed, dreams that came true. I was plagued with dreams, most in the form of a trilogy that were prophetic and ominous–one such futuristic dream haunts me still–I see its ramifications everywhere I look...

I was in a stone tower, located far above the land, dressed in some medieval type clothing; pouring over some ancient bound book. It was nighttime and there were candles lit on the shelves and on the table I stood at. Suddenly I heard screaming, plaintive screeching howls, coming from below my tower. I ran to the window to see what was happening and when I looked out, I saw the entire world below me. Everywhere people were looking up at the skies with their hands clutching at their hearts and mouths. I looked up to see what they were frightened of, hoping it was just some kind of comet, or perhaps falling stars. What I saw instead was a stark, slow procession of stars, all together, leaving us and the skies behind. In their wake was nothing but a severe black sky; no planets, no stars, just deep sorrowful inky black darkness.

The sorrow that dream left me with lasted for days. It was such a loss; the feeling of something beautiful gone, never to be replaced. I did not know if it was a portent or maybe even a memory but when I think of what's happening to our world now that, dream always comes to mind.

Dreams like that don't come often, but when they do, your whole body knows it; your skin reacts as though every cell had just received a shot of mystical insulin; tingling, alive, anticipatory, knowing something wiser and greater than you just touched your soul. They were definitely not spiritual in the sense that I had been taught–yet they were far more spiritual anything I had ever heard of by that time. I kept them to myself knowing instinctively they were not meant to be shared with priest, nun, or even parent. I cannot tell you how I knew they were a calling, but I knew!

I honestly do not feel I was unique in this childhood sense of wonder and faith, as most Pagans I know had the same early sense of the mystical. Truly, all children have a strong, innate sense of faith in something greater than themselves–a sense that doesn't have to be beaten into them, or beefed up with scary stories of those who underwent torturous, dramatic, and painful deaths just to prove their faith in God–it's natural to children. Although I loved Joan of Arc, it wasn't because of her faith in God. It was due to her sense of bravery and commitment to a purpose she felt so intrinsic to her world–I actually found myself wanting to avenge her death!

As with all of us, the trouble began to seep in as I began to stretch my wings and ran smack into the face of dogma; the Priests and Dominican Nuns of St. Alphonsus grade school and Holy Angels high school. It was not so much the teachings of Catholicism–i.e. that God was the only face of divinity, absolute and ready to clobber us anytime we got out of line, anytime we wavered in our faith–but how the acceptance of that dogma began to crush the magic, the sense of mystery in my life that left me with a sense of depression, and constant anxiety.

Truthfully, I loved all the mystic greatness of my faith; I believed in loving and honoring some huge force that had created all the wonder and awe of life; but I hated all the torture, pain, servitude and bleakness that apparently was the stuff and stamina of all those iconic

8

saints who lived it. So, there you have it. Love and hate, bred by faith, education and fate; life was pain and death was great! What's a girl to do?

It took me a long time after severing ties with the church and its dogma, as well as the snarky cynical attitude I adopted, to realize that the guilt I carried was far less about the break with a religious faith than it was about the break of faith in the magic, the mystery, the awe, grace and beauty of life itself. It took a long time to understand that the faith and awe I felt as a young girl had nothing at all to do with religion! It was my natural state. Faith all too often becomes confused with religion and dogma–what a tragedy.

It was also about that time (around 12) that St. Al's (the affectionate name we gave our grade school) gave one of its spiritual retreats–no school, just lectures from the nuns and priests about becoming one of them. Sometime during the third day an extraordinary thing occurred that, although I could not have known at that time, would show up in my life as a pattern, just like the dreams; I think of them both as the part of my awakening.

I became smitten; I fell in love with the idea of giving myself to God, becoming a nun, offering my life to this great one heavenly father. I began walking forward to pledge myself and suddenly felt someone grab me by the hair on my head, pull me back and literally throw me against an invisible wall. Yet there was no one there, there wasn't even a wall. I was so shaken I immediately sat back down; someone, something was there beside me, arresting me, and it wasn't human! But I felt it, it touched me; scary, unreal, yet impossibly real. Later, I could grasp a sense of what it was; I knew it was a 'she'; that she was protective and wise, and somehow knew me better than I knew myself. Once again, I knew I couldn't share the experience with any authority; especially since she had an attitude of no Saint Theresa. I wish I could give you some definitive explanation for what had occurred—without turning into a raving, first year psyche major, but I can't. I can only tell you that I now know she was/is my inner goddess/guide. Mostly she appears to be laughing or dancing; a very large boned, large breasted woman, bare feet sticking out under a dark full skirt, necklaces made from wood, nuts and twigs, wild gray hair flying amuck, and, weirdly enough, sucking on a cheroot. I'm not even sure what a cheroot is, I just know she loves them. I believe now that her actions came about due to an "in between lives" pact I made, about not choosing to become a nun, yet again, in this lifetime. Apparently, I had spent far too many lives as a nun—enough!

Holy Angels was an "all-girls" Catholic high school. Our nuns were almost a caricature of every horror tale told—demanding suffocation, devotion & obedience; they suffered unbearably from their own oppression with such glee that I suppose they were trying to show us how beatific it was. Our biology teacher could not speak about the body without blushing, huge red spots would appear on her face, and she was barely able to breathe. We sat there immobilized throughout her weepy break down. Then she would try to explain how to take a Christian bath without touching or gazing too long on any particular spots. Our home room nun did have a break down—two of them–and ended up in a mental ward for two of our 4 years together. The principal smiled, rubbing her hands together when you did something wrong–yeah, punishment was coming! One year I spent so much time in the chapel asking for forgiveness that I nearly flunked algebra.

The whiplash us girls felt between the nuns' attitude of slap, slam and wham and the saint's inspirational heroic, steadfast, devotion was just simply painful–like being horribly thirsty yet having one's mouth covered with tape. Which in fact, actually did happen in the 8th grade–I spent recess with my mouth taped for getting out of line, something I did quite often.

It would be years before I understood what had happened to those women, what made them so dark and unforgiving; they lived the life of an abused Housewife, believing that any indignation they might have would only prove them unworthy. They needed to take their abuse out on anyone who colored outside the lines. How easy it was, and still is, to link abuse, pain and oppression to spirituality, all in the name of God.

I eventually gave up on my Catholic lineage, something to do with the inevitable fallout from spiritual terrorism, not to mention 12 years hard time with religious neurosis, saddle shoe and navy blue uglies, and the pious passivity that surrounded it all. Years went by as I tried to reshape the face of God, redefine, color and liberalize his words so they'd fit–I know that right here we're supposed to say 'bring some meaning to life', but that was my problem. Life didn't need meaning; it was spirituality that needed meaning. No matter how I tried to fix it, it began to resemble an old car, Monday you fix the radiator and Tuesday the brakes go out; you just can't fit a wild pagan heart into an old-timey black book.

Other than the occasional jolt in and out of the dream dimensions and strange mysticism that occurred, growing up for me had all the normal teenager's struggles and joys, odd jobs (I once was paid in doughnuts, literally) longing for boyfriends, girlfriends and bla bla bla. My family was your normal run-of-mill family with 10 children and, therefore, we had a whole lot of survival issues. None of which matched 'Ozzie & Harriet or Leave It To Beaver!'

# Chapter 3–A Small Café, a Huge Miracle

Eventually, I moved to Texas and entered a 10-year common-law relationship with Andy. He was all Irish, second generation Philadelphia stock, whiskey breath, ruddy face with an "I gotcha" kind of smile. He was my hero; a tough Union man, an idealistic sort who swore he'd never back down in the face of injustice. I watched with horror when he did just that, believing the Union let him down. He never got up again without the help of a bottle and the memory of his slow, desolate crawl from the pieces of a shattered dream remained with me always. I learned one great thing from Andy; the only way to keep a dream from shattering is to never forget that it came from you.

The next 5 years was a series of slow-motion breakdowns: Andy grew from a loving, idealistic Irish lover to a raging belligerent drunk; I moved like a sleepwalker trying to hold on, let go, fix, run, scream until I almost dissolved. One day, standing by the window I started to cry; my goddess/guide showed up again: Get Out, Get Out she screamed. I started making plans, but I guess just wasn't ready yet to let go completely; surely there was some way to save this relationship. In between drunken states I managed to coax him towards the direction I wanted. He sold the house and we took the money to Flagstaff, Arizona and bought a run-down, inhospitable burger joint for the fantastic sum of $6,000.

It was called the Snack Shack; a 24-hour, 10 to 1# frozen burger patties, brick chili (just add water, no seasoning needed) dump whose clientele came from the many bars around town that catered to the Hopi and Navajo Indians hooked on drugs and alcohol. It was an old-timey trailer with the grill out front, L-shaped counter, 4 booths and in the back, a tiny storage room. I remember peeing in the toilet once, turning around to flush and there, staring at me in the bowl, was a tiny mouse looking up as if to say 'what just happened?' We had no idea how bad it was till we took over. I tried so many times to introduce myself to the business people around town, explaining that the Snack Shack had new owners who were going to clean it up, serve great delicious food, but always it was the same response:

"Yes, well," always followed by a sweet limp hand shake, "hope you make a go of it, good luck, but we never frequent the place."

This was not part of a journey I thought I'd ever take, if indeed, I ever thought I'd take a journey at all–I didn't even know how to cook, that was his expertise! But looking back on it, it was beautifully choreographed–the high mountain desert of Northern Arizona, the mystery and awe of the Hopi Mesas, the Grand Canyon lands, Canyon DeChelle, Sedona, and the phoenix rising of Kathy's Café; they were all going to play a pivotal role in my journey!

Things at the café were not going well–things like coming in for my shift and finding that Andy had spent the entire time playing poker and drinking with his best new buddies, or the time when four ladies, waiting for the train, had ordered pancakes...he made one enormous cake on the grill, then split it four ways, pizza style and served them with a smile. They laughed; of course, how could you ignore his dimpled grin? I cried.

An incident occurred however, during this time which shook me to the core. It wasn't anything to do with everyday life, the café, or my growing anxiety with Andy and yet it triggered within me a shift in perspective that was powerful–my inner volcano had begun to rise.

We were invited to the Hopi Mesas for their sacred Snake Dance in Hotevilla. The Snake Dance is the culmination of days of prayer and fasting within the Kivas for the purpose of bringing forth the rains. It was probably best that I didn't fully grasp the power and sacredness of this invitation; I would have had an agenda, fully developed in my mind alone and most likely would have been disappointed if it hadn't been fulfilled. As it was, I was unprepared and astounded.

We spent the night in a tent outside our Host's home. Andy brought some whiskey and I was painfully aware of the solemnity of their request to not bring liquor on the reservation. After we were busted, I was painfully ashamed! My own inability to stand up to what was the right thing to do was so weak…that was what made me so ashamed.

The next day we joined the village in the square. Everyone was seated upon old stone steps or wood beams that formed the roof tops to their stone mesa homes. I looked around at a semi-circle of cowboy hats and boots, long brightly colored skirts and mismatched blouses; thick, heavy, blue/black hair, turquoise belts, squash blossoms and silver ornaments and felt totally out of place. Moments later, four wizened Hopi priests emerged from the Kiva, which to me looked like a sunken tomb. I was smitten immediately, listening to the sound of the rattle, the drum and the beat of a chant meant for creature and human alike; I could almost feel the soft leather of their tunics, their fringe, tassels and beads. I could feel a power building up all around me. I didn't know what it was, but I could feel it, nevertheless.

Four young, strapping Hopi boys then came and released the snakes. Live snakes. Rattlesnakes. Emissaries of the earth who would speak to the spirits, I assumed. For at least an hour, four snakes, four priests moved around each other with the mutual respect of adversarial dancers who had only one stage on which to perform. The final step of this strange dance was a kiss! Each priest gently raising a snake, and mouth to mouth, began praying, swaying, speaking to it: "please go to the four corners and ask the spirits to release the rain."

My mind went numb, thankfully, leaving me nothing to do but feel what was happening. I was fully present, fully experiencing, allowing myself to simply breathe in every sense around me. I think, that was what triggered the shift within.

Apparently, an agreement had been made. The snakes crawled towards the north, south, east and west; the priests returned to the Kiva and the people began to prepare for the celebration of the rains they knew would come. One day later, it was raining.

I remember, afterwards, munching on some blue corn piki bread on the ride back home, how the questions began hurling themselves inside and outside my head. Now I wanted to think, needed to think, to question;

wanted to leave the mystical, return to reality; reach out for the mystical, run back to reality, and question, question, question. Had the snakes been milked? Was it all symbolic, just a bunch of pet snakes; peyote, priests and drugged up snakes? I wandered aimlessly inside my head and my logic, bouncing back and forth between elation and cynicism, all the while listening to the hot dry sounds of an Arizona Mesa, come to life Brigadoon, in the year of our Lord, late 1970-something.

At some point, I began to fully understand the ramifications of that day; what was so humbling, breathless and exciting. There, all around me was an outward demonstration of the belief in unity, of oneness, of the connection of all life. Was it that belief alone which made it possible for rattler and human to communicate without strike? To come together in peace for the good of all? Could the result of such a belief bring forth a miracle...like the rains that came for the Hopi, or perhaps, the reign of peace on a planet, just for the good of all? I had questions, lots of them, but I didn't mind it. I couldn't answer these questions, I just simply knew they held a deep everlasting truth within them.

The Hopi are Matriarchal; I didn't understand then what 'Matriarchal' meant other than the lands and lineage passed through the woman. I understood only that it was different from our patriarchal, male centered world. It would be years before I understood that the main difference was in their Goddess-centered beliefs that all life, not just human life, was sacred and equal; and their spiritual beliefs in their Gods and Goddesses which was so strong it made it possible for them to cross the veil of communication between mankind, animal and the elements. I couldn't verbalize it then, but awakening within me was a deep desire to have that same strength in my life; it had the feel of an ancient memory begging to be brought forth.

I also awakened to another realization, a very sad realization. Between us living within our own carefully structured belief system, there was a bond—a kind of unwritten agreement- to simply disbelieve, or ignore, any belief that does not support our own. Not everyone succumbed to that bond, but most of society did. And those of us who did not, still suffered with the back and forth fight between what was an unconscious agreement, and our new found desire to grasp something greater. I certainly was then.

Even with all the hype and media feeding off the Hopi/Navajo relocation struggle, I knew this tiny nation had lived in peace for centuries. With all our technology, with all our churches, throughout all the history of our religions and governments, we have never been able to accomplish such a miracle. Somehow it didn't seem very likely we ever would since we've been around this planet for as long as they have. How did they do it? How is it that we have not?

The next day found me back in my usual drama, the one I could really relate to; busying myself with every day worries about the cafe. But to be perfectly honest, underlying everything I did from that day on was a sense of awe and wonder to what I had witnessed on the Hopi Reservation–I could not forget it.

Within a year, Andy landed in jail for numerous DWIs, assaults, a hit and run on a police officer's wife–he was on the move again! At that time, any property or business purchased by an unmarried couple went into the name of the man only, so I had to go to court, determined to take sole ownership of the Snack Shack. I still remember the snide remark by the judge,

"Why would anyone want to fight for that piece of junk?"

It was one of those defining moments in life; I couldn't walk away, it was all I had left, there was nowhere to go, we had to get a common-law divorce so the café could become mine legally and I did so gratefully. Even now, though, telling people I was divorced long before I ever married has really been fun!

So that piece of junk café was to become my life, my lover, my child. I knew so little about starting a business, had so little training in the scriptures of success that I believe that's what saved me–when I lost all my help, counted up the miserable $75 a day sale, I never thought I was failing, just a little slow. I threw out the building inspector because he told me the place was a disaster; tossed out many men and women, including a bit too drunk Navajo man, an ex-football player who wanted to sleep in a bowl of chili–I grabbed a hold of him and we both went flying out the door and collided together into a pancake on the sidewalk just as a possible customer went walking by. He stepped over us without so much as a by-your-leave!

I hired a dishwasher to help out; a rolly polly, GI haircut, overweight "Bobby" who was incredibly eager to work. He must have worked for over a month when he came to me, wringing his hands, shifting from baggy pant leg to baggy pant leg.

"Um, I was just wondering, if it's O.K., could I have a day off sometime, I mean, if it's O.K.?"

I was so embarrassed; my 7 day a week virus infected work ethics didn't allow me to think about days off!

Then there was Gretchen, my first waitress, from Alaska...a great lady! And a great story; she was tall, large boned, long brown hair and stood ramrod straight, and had a grace about her that would have sent the royal cats of Egypt to shame. She had been working with a hunter in Alaska, high up in his mountain camp, cut off from any other humans for a solid year. Until suddenly she felt the need to leave and reconnect with who she was as a woman. On coming back and needing work, she simply pictured herself working at a small café and then found herself standing in front of mine. Once, when we were busy, I was flipping eggs, hash browns and pancakes and didn't realize John Denver had come in and sat down at the counter. I was not a great fan of his, so had none of his music. He asked Gretchen if there were any and she replied:

"I'm so sorry, Mr. Denver. We get our music from the thrift shops and I guess no one ever turns in yours!" She really was a dream.

There were so many wild times then, running out of fry-bread dough with a line of people waiting for more; Andy, when released from jail threatening everyone, tossing them out, stealing two checks from the back of the checkbook and wiping out my account; cooks taking the money, drunks still demanding for a booth to sleep in and chili to puke in; a megalomania man-monster swiping the French fries from someone ease's plate who transformed me into a superwoman–I literally picked him up from the front of his shirt and threw him against the wall before tossing him out–when I was angry I tended to move toward very dangerous, but self-assured actions! Then of course, there was the customer who asked me to save his coffee–"I'll be right back"–and went down the street, entered the local bar and shot the bartender dead!

But there were also so many magical times, all us women new to business, working together during the lean dry times, hiring the children, supporting each other. The stroke of genius that came out of nowhere that led to my "Menu Burning Parties"; when the menus got too old and scruffy, or I had to increase prices it became a hot-roaring celebration for my customers! Soon it all started to work, things came together, customers came in daily...daily! I couldn't believe it. I sponsored a street fair, had poetry readings; college students and Professors began meeting there–people were talking about and frequenting The Snack Shack! Until it all fell apart again. I lost the lease and felt as though someone had stuck a knife into me.

I wandered around for days, in a daze, flipping back and forth between desperation to do something, anything, and the strong pit-of the-stomach need to crawl into bed and cry. Finally, I went to see some friends who had a small deli/health food store on San Francisco Street. They informed me they needed to sell the building and would I like to buy? I thought the earth just opened up her arms and embraced me with all the grace in the world!

There was so much maneuvering going on at that time it made my head spin! I had to borrow money just to get a down-payment, make loans I had no way to pay back; re-construct the kitchen, the building, buy tables; with no income coming in it was a whirlwind of faith. I lost money to a contractor who started the job then fled; went to court with a plumber who went on a binge and didn't show for weeks, then sued me because I hired another plumber to finish the job. I was sued so many times during that fiasco that I just got used to walking into the lawyer's office, signing the papers with a smile and walking out with a 'you'll get the money soon–very soon'.

Then one day it happened. The Snack Shack died and Kathy's Café was born; soft pastels surrounded the booths and wood tables spread all around, sky-lights in both rooms, 2 potbelly wood stoves, one in each room, a beautifully carved arched doorway leading into the smaller room, two grills, two sinks and one huge rose painted clear across the outside of the building like a flag, a symbol, a declaration. I had no idea then why I was so attracted to the Rose, but I should have known, it was and always had been a symbol for the Goddess I was yet unaware of, but always there beside me.

It was such a journey, those years at the café, not just learning how to wiggle out of financial tight spots, but learning about the bond that exists in the simple pleasures of gathering people together to eat and share food. Learning the language of food, the scents and instincts of its spices and tastes. Kathy's became a place to gather and hatch ideas, dreams, stories; to meet and greet others you may not meet otherwise. I loved it.

Bursting behind all this grace, however, I soon developed a restlessness, an incomplete feeling I couldn't put a finger on. At times it left me vacant, empty, disconnected. Sometimes I felt as though I was shifting, dodging inside, turning slowly like a slackening top; brewing like stale coffee. During those times, there were two things that would still the restlessness and awaken a sense of awe and joy–the Hopi Mesas and Mexico.

Whenever I needed to find room to breathe, but had a short period of time, I'd drive to the Mesas; a stone's throw from Flagstaff, but light years away in spirit. Something inside woke up just by being there; an awareness that seemed to come up gulping for air each time it got close to nature. It left me feeling alive, brand new, some kind of Ms. Heart and Mr. Mind meets, falls in love and lives happily ever after sort of feeling. Stepping onto those matriarchal, grandmother lands, I could feel an emanation of energy beam all around me, as if the land itself was beaming, laughing and prancing. Her fat, red gold hills dressed in green skirted valleys roaming free, anywhere and everywhere they wanted; her high tipped spires and low flat mesas looking a lot like high pointed nipples and well worked bellies; looking a lot like the essence of a beautiful woman, independent, willful, proud and purposeful–I was burning alive with her beauty! On the drive up there, I felt that if I stuck my hand out the window and grabbed, I would be able to grab onto that essence, as though the air contained it and the land could speak it; as though words like peace, simplicity, unity,

23

harmony were only guttural translations of its language. I loved that language and wanted to learn it. If I could speak it, perhaps I could make it come true. I began to understand one of the greatest gifts of nature–learning through osmosis–a gift of absorbing wisdom through the energy and instinct of a greater world around you. While gawking at a rainbow, watching a squirrel jump limb to limb, or a whale fluke slap at the water, the seeds of knowledge and wisdom quietly slip past all the tapes and judgments of the mind and are lovingly planted within the womb of your heart waiting for you to bring the words into the world. Quite simply put, she is a sentient being, and every time you step into her womb, sentience is the ultimate gift she gives to you!

Mexico held the much the same energy for me, albeit a bit more fiery. My love and connection to her began with a trip to the Yucatan. Just stepping out of the plane I felt as though I was returning home again to some ancient matriarchal paradise. The smells, the scents and beauty of that peninsula, fringed with ocean, covered with jungle; ancient history of cultures long since disappeared, yet somehow, I felt so close to. the Mayans became as real to me as my own lineage. Isle Mujeres was a home and Playa Del Carmen a romance–with a fisherman, in a hammock on the beach, under the full moon and only a few stars who were able to make it past her light to witness our embrace.

I loved my café, it was my lover, my child, my life; but something was missing. It was the kind of empty, disconnection one feels that can't be tricked by a shopping spree, a record customer day, or even a fervent day of prayer. It was a lack that could only be filled by going deeper into that spiritual dimension that lives on so many levels around us.

# Chapter 4–Play to Pray!

Soon I began to explore other spiritual teachings, some have been called cultist, but each one gave me one more piece of the puzzle. No matter how insightful however, they all flowed from and returned to a male God, with his hierarchical way of explaining spirituality. I still felt as though something was missing. Yet there was a marvelous delight in dipping in and out of each one that leaves you living a kind of 'Dorothy in Oz-ness'–part of you lives in black and white and the other in living, shrieking Technicolor. All my life the Wizard of Oz was just possibly my most favorite movie; my admiration for it greatly increased when I began to understand the message to all girls cleverly disguised within it. Just think about it, way back in the 1900's—long before the women's empowerment movement—L. Frank Baum publishes a book about a young farm girl whisked away to another world, going about saving this world from a wicked witch, emboldening the mind of a scarecrow, opening up the heart of a tin man, hearkening the courage of a cowardly lion, and then finally revealing the little man behind the mask of a narcissistic wizard for all to see! I like to ponder about where Baum got his ideas; a prophetic dream? A wise old grandmother? Wherever it was, he was so ahead of his time.

A year or so later however, I was to experience a solid, direct hit, complete with Technicolor, extraordinary senses, indefinable communication and touch that made me realize what exactly was missing in these spiritual teachings. It spun me around as though I was nothing more than a rubber kneed rag doll. It was a moment imprinted forever on my mind and body.

I was in Santa Barbara and had just finished a large step on the ladder of the spiritual teachings I was taking. The day began with an incredible gratitude for being alive, permeated with love, with life, and a childlike sense of play—the state of mind that drives you to reach out to all sorts of beings, real or imagined; drives you to pet kittens, as well as snakes, and just as importantly, drives you to serve hot fudge sundaes for dinner as a vegetable. I suppose it began where it always begins!

There was not much to do that afternoon so my buddy Steve and I took off to the beach, each deciding to go our own way and meet back at the car at sunset. It was that incredible pre-sunset hour when Earth begins to change into her ball gown colors, deeper and richer than any color should be. I loved it! The beach was deserted, strangely enough, and the sand was seductive—grab it, stick it between your toes, on your knees—all that giggly stuff you do when surrendering yourself to play. And I did and did again—kick the can, hide and seek. I played with the sun, the color purple washing in with the waves and the rocks littered all around the shore. It seemed as though I had stumbled into a precocious moment, a perfect world. As questionable, loony, and irrational it may seem, as New Agey, fanatical and out-there it may seem, suddenly I knew something was playing with me! I could feel it—moving around me, peeping over my shoulder, laughing as I stumbled over shells, got tangled in seaweed or distracted by a nosy gull. I'd turn, pretending to catch it and it would quite obviously disappear. Yet it, or they, or something was there, teasing, matching mood for mood, as silly and playful as I was. Crazy? I didn't care; nothing, nothing mattered except this wild ecstatic moment. Time slid by on its tummy, running back and forth between first base and home plate until sunset. It was time to go.

I started back, but couldn't get away. Couldn't leave until I had said…I don't know, bye, or thanks, or something, but what? There had to be words to acknowledge whatever or whoever this was. I ran over and jumped on a large flat boulder close to the red mounds strung along the periphery and decided to just say it all. I love you. I see you. I'll be back. Blah blah blah. That's when everything I knew as real began to break apart–no matter how many times we tell ourselves the impossible is real, actually experiencing it always leaves us flat on our backs.

There was movement. An undercurrent, like the slow but steady pulse of drums, far away but getting closer and closer. Without warning, something touched me from behind, from the front, from every angle; the pressure of a strong, almost smothering embrace began caressing the top of my head, my face, my back, legs and hands. Everywhere an invisible touch was enveloping and enfolding my whole body. With every pressing hug, with every touch, came the most powerful sense of love I had ever felt, before or since; as though the essence of love itself had broken away from some prehistoric boundary just to take form, just to hold someone in its arms. It held me there. I was breathless, unable to speak, to move; held up, petrified and liquefied in ecstasy. I was a mess. A happy, ecstatic, shocked mess. Slowly it began to retreat, seemingly taking hours before its last delicate substance was gone, floating away through the debris of what once was thought to be substantial. I was so bewildered, so grateful–how could something this enormous happen right here in this real world we live in daily? The hair was still rising on the back of my neck as I walked away, trying not to think, breathing in every last detail of a moment I could hardly believe. I finally reached the car and saw Steve.

Steve was my best buddy and intellectual dueling partner. I cannot begin to tell you how many restaurants we had closed while arguing everything from Hitler to his current lover. He had absolutely no sense of romance or intimate survival. While he was willing to admit to the needs of his partner, it always came from thinking, from knowing what should be done, never from instinct or because he just wanted to buy a gift or bring flowers. Never would I have expected to see him carrying what he had in his hand right then–a fat bouquet of wild flowers–I had never even seen him holding a Christmas gift before! Handing them over, he said:

"I think these must be for you. Can't imagine why I'd get an urge to pick flowers. Strangest thing. Here, take them. You don't suppose..."

I knew. Every sense I had told me I knew who and where they had come from, but I just couldn't let it be, couldn't stop myself. Horrified, I watched as I did one of the most devastating things I have ever done in my life.

"Steve, do you think it's possible that the Earth, or nature, well, that maybe it has a spirit self, or can take shape, talk to us, touch us?"

He began in his unquiet, predictable way–logic spewing forth, logic begetting logic, logic ripping thru any anomaly worthy of its name–until I could no longer hear his negation. Any attention I had left was being torn apart by the sound of my heart, breaking, into a million pieces. It was the sound of ugly metallic rational fingers scratching out the possibility of what had just occurred; leaving behind the sound of cold steel walls slamming shut; leaving behind a flat, still life replica to replace a living, breathing precious moment. My doubt, my need to question what happened left me wracked with an unbearable sense of betrayal. I was SCREAMING inside.

"Thanks Steve, these are beautiful" I said.

"Yeah, well. I need to think about this." He turned, scratching his head at the anomaly that had sent him picking wildflowers.

I cannot tell you how many times I have thought of that day, how many questions it has spun–why is it so easy to toss aside the magic of life, why are we so afraid of it; how can we experience something, then turn around and question whether or not it happened; is it truly logical to doubt something so beautiful to the point we literally shut down our ability to see it? Do we really have to lose an experience before it becomes truly impactful? I thought again of that strange, unspoken, unhealthy bond we have that entrenches us in the need to reject anything supernatural, anything that cannot be explained with logic. Are we really so shallow?

Is play, trust, surrender, a secret key to slipping into the unknown life forces that exist on Earth? After that experience, I knew without a doubt that there were/are dimensions on Earth, dimensions of Earth herself–is play a tool for parting the veil to these dimensions?

Earth seems to hold secrets that somehow could be known with just a slight shift in our energy, and play and laughter almost always brings on an enormous shift. With that shift, at that moment I held a key to those secrets in my hands that I had never held before, sealed with a kiss, topped off with a bouquet of twigs, toasted green leaves, yellow butter cups and dandelions! Whatever I had connected with wanted it as much as I did. Whatever it was, it was sentient. Whatever I connected with expressed more love than anything I had experienced before, including all the spiritual teachings I had ever before experienced. It was real. That makes no sense. I understand that. So I can only offer this–it was an experience my soul will always remember, an expression of the Spiritual and temporal that was real, even though everything we experience as real would prove it to be an hallucination. But it wasn't. It was the kind of spirituality I wanted to roll around the grass with, make friends with, express deeply in my life and I so needed to get closer to it.

There was a kind of underground shift going on with me after that incident. I canceled the rest of the training I was taking then simply because, beyond a doubt, I knew there was not enough love within it, it was wrong somehow. All my previous experiences at Hopi land began to make more sense–the energy I could sense coming from the land, the feminine sense of the land; the connection the Hopis had with creatures and elements. There was something so much greater going on here on Earth and something missing in our thinking, and in our connection to Her. Maybe it's a tribute to that 'sisterhood' link between Earth and women that makes it more likely for women to understand or feel this, maybe there are secrets about a woman's soul that brings us closer to the soul of Earth, and whatever all that means. I wasn't sure what any of this meant, but soon enough I began to sense the need to move on, to start reaching out for the signs of this connection. Not too much later, I got the strongest urge to put my beloved café up for sale, buy a boat and go live on the ocean. Go figure.

# The Guide Speaks

Spirituality is inherent, a natural aspect of self and one's own spiritual path—which cannot be determined by anyone else! There are vast consequences of teaching dogma that serves to undermine the integrity of one's path, and consequences to accepting that dogma. For centuries, women have had their path chosen for them—with devastating results. The invisible walls that have been constructed around a woman's spiritual integrity are enormous; BUT they are also breakable—because metaphorically and realistically, through the Summons, every woman gets her chance to break the bonds! Some of you will close your ears, put it down to hogwash and end up the sister, wife, daughter or nun, giving credit to the brother, priest, the father and Son for what you alone can see···until you can see no more; you will dismiss responsibility for what you alone can feel, until you can feel no more—all questions and answers neatly tied up and delivered through the hands of authority. Some of you will jump for joy, and be amazed with the mystery you have just stepped into. That is when you can grab your chance to face the Moon and learn once again to speak your Mother Tongue. That is when you will find your way back to your own inherent spiritual self. But you must unplug from what has been handed to you—and that is not always easy—because then you must learn to live with the consequence of 'knowing'.

# Chapter 5-Grace of the Ocean

I should probably say this right now, and get it over with. The idea of being alone at sea began to frighten the heck out of me. I wish I could tell you I was brave and bold and went out the next day to purchase a 42' sailing craft. I didn't. I began to think of solutions to my fear (when will we ever learn that the solution to fear can only bring more fear?) and the best one I thought of was to get married, have someone near and dear to my heart to share the dream with. The fact that I didn't have anyone near and dear to my heart didn't seem to enter into the equation. He'll be there, he has to, or else this isn't going to happen. And guess what–he showed up! I would not attempt to tell you if this was a mistake or not–we had an enormously challenging relationship–but I know that his presence helped to make the 1st part of my journey happen. And for that I am grateful. Still, I would have to face sailing alone later, it wasn't going to go away.

Wayne G. A great man. As happy as he was large. A hot shot contractor who wore pink shirts a lot because a good-looking sales lady told him he looked sexy in them (she was right!). Soft brown hair and brown eyes, and he laughed as much as he could! He loved life in the fast lane, yet through it all, remained a romantic wuss when it came to weddings. I was number four. Someone he never before met the likes of. Someone who just swept him off his feet with dreams of sailing the ocean, talk of herbal cures, mysticism and a whole host of wonders he had never thought of before. So we bound our souls together, in what was probably the strangest matrimonial ceremony he ever partook in–he was both minister and participant, no official witnesses, although we forged their names, one of which was Merlin Emery's. We sent off the renegade document and received a bonafide certificate. I haven't a clue as to the statement we were trying to make, but I'm sure at the time there was one. Afterwards we sold our businesses and charged off to the world of sailors, barnacles, and the boat of our dreams–a 47' stay sail ketch in Florida we re-blessed, redressed and renamed "Merlin". Of course. So began our rocky relationship. We had started with outrageous flirting and simply never got any deeper–at least not recognizably so–what happened, happened underneath all the glitz and garble of our lives.

I'd like to share a story with you about Merlin–a figure who was dear to me since childhood. On one of the lonely drives back from California, among the eternal rolling hills and long stretches of flat gray road, and before the events in Santa Barbara, I challenged that spirit to an imaginary duel of magic.

"Wake up Merlin. I know you're out there somewhere in this universe!" I swear he answered with a sudden, out of nowhere, double rainbow. I jumped out of the car and tossed back a challenge of dragons made from clouds, then dragon eyes that he flashed open and I closed. We dueled back and forth in the middle of a wide-open Arizona sky for what seemed like a half hour. Then suddenly between one moment to the next, between my natural instinct to explore the depths of every possible dimension that might exist and that severe, cautionary instinct we all seem to hold on to, it began to feel scary; goose-bump kind of scary and all I could think of was–if this was real, maybe I shouldn't fool around with it. Now what I think about is–just how much magic do we hold within our fingertips? What could we do if we realized our full potential? So, yes, Merlin was a big part of mine, then Wayne's lives.

Wayne seemed happy then to be a part of my idiosyncrasies. We spent nearly a year outfitting Merlin; on a short sail outside Florida's harbor we had a knockdown and tore the sails to shreds. No matter, they were replaced with the most beautiful red sails we could find–set against her black mast she was looking gorgeous! On another sail we tore up the engine, it got replaced. She was outfitted with a new dingy, deck boxes; we polished the teak, inside and out, replaced the galley ware, cushions, installed a refrigeration system and took pictures every step of the way until the camera broke. Finally, after it seemed as though we'd never get away we crammed every nook and crawl space with food & supplies; bought charts that would get us all the way to Venezuela, and suddenly, we were one pizza, one night away from untying the lines and slipping away from the dock.

Just before we took off, we got this notion to bring along with us those areas of life we had only dabbled in before, or secretly wanted to; art, music, meditation, massage and tarot cards. He bought a harmonica and a keyboard; I loaded up with paints, how-to books and a guitar, then went looking for the cards. I walked into this sweet-smelling book shop where incense, oils, and herbs mingled with books, tattletale palmist and all sorts of fun stuff. I have always been fond of books that fall off the shelf as you walk by, or people you slam into on the street who become a customer the next day…and you don't even have to apologize for what you were thinking, and that's the sort of thing that happened here. Of course! I found a deck of Merlin cards, took them of the shelf, thinking–hey! This was meant to be! But then, turning towards the register, a set of round tarot cards called "Mother Peace", written by Vicki Noble, caught my eye. They didn't exactly fall off the shelf, but they held me, frozen solid, in place. I couldn't get away, couldn't stop looking at them. They felt like a deep blue well of spring water I wanted to dive into. Honestly, I could not move away. Finally, I looked at the Merlin deck in my hand and knew I had to let it go. I reached for the round cards and knew I had made the right decision–a Woman called the Goddess had just entered my life, and while I was no feminist, I knew she was meant to be there.

Our first stop was to be Bimini, in the Bahamas and we made the crossing from Florida right on the edge of a storm. Our first, but not to be our last. It was harrowing; it was the first visit from the Dark Mother of the Ocean. The next day we pulled into the Custom dock at Bimini, checked in then went ashore for dinner. A supposed, and hopefully fabulous dinner to celebrate our new life. I threw up all over the gardens outside the restaurant; not because of the food, but because every edge of nervous energy I had been holding onto for the last year just seemed to explode from my mouth;  I was doubled over with cramps, puking every step of the way back to the boat. A disgusting and revolting beginning!

By the next day I was fully purged and truly ready to go. Our sail thru the tiny islands of the Bahamas was like a sail thru fairy lands–each little islet was a jewel dropped from the heavens, with Rays jumping in the water, fish darting in and out, and at night, anchored in a quiet cove I began to realize how vast and magical life could be if we just surrendered to it. But more than that I began to feel the spiritual essence of Mother Earth & Sister Ocean.

While the cruising life is no easy way to find women's awareness books, it's the best way I know of to get back to your women's awareness. Mother Nature moves in real close and sits down right next to you, whispering in your ear, opening up your eyes. You hear her thoughts, she becomes your T.V., your newscaster, until suddenly you seem surrounded by a whole host of Feminine Pedagogues older and wiser than you and you feel touched by spirit. That's what it felt like to me, every mystical cell in my body was becoming inexorably intertwined with this ocean essence; building a home inside my heart until every breath became a particle of its wholeness.

Somewhere between the Bahamas and St. Thomas, our next destination, I settled down to read the book that accompanied my round Tarot cards. That may have been the beginning of mine and Wayne's crumbling relationship. I came face to face with Matriarchy and the idea of a Mother Goddess who stood on Her own, neither subject to, nor a mimic of, a father God. She demanded balance in a world they believed they were both a part of. To Wayne however, the once to be preacher, it was totally irrational. Something I would read would trigger a whole avalanche of ideas and he'd rare back like the Taurus he was and start shouting:

"This is ridiculous! How can you just believe all this crap?"

Those were the times the arguments became down and dirty. He found himself fighting a battle he never intended to allow in his life. He was an ex-Baptist and had been trained as a preacher (I wanted to be a nun at one time, actually we were a good match). His training as a preacher never guided his career choices, but they did guide his spiritual choices. He was fine with the idea of Merlin and mystical happenings, they were interesting, non-threatening. But a woman stepping in, claiming a part of creation, a say in the voice of spirituality; it was simply not to be.

"This is bull-shit; it's just a book that means nothing at all." He'd clamp the wheel tighter and tighter as he spoke.

To me she felt like rich silk, a siren red slip–wiggle into it and watch it raise dead nipples on a 100-year-old crone. For the first time in my life, spirituality made sense; you really could step outside the church walls and roll around in the grass with it. You really could hear words that were part of a feminine heritage. I knew almost nothing about that heritage. Yet it was a heritage, an essence and feeling that was as familiar to me as my family name; its familiarity was bubbling up from inside at the rate of a flood.

Yet there were times when, while spending many days under sail, pouring through the cards like kids playing with a forbidden toy that I knew Wayne really loved them. He'd pick one up and laugh.

"This is great! Look at this guy, what I'd give to approach life like that!"

It became his favorite card, the Son of Wands, a jester who loved laughter, people and life. He seemed to melt right inside it, one hand on the wheel of Merlin, one hand on a card from the Goddess; a man peeking out from behind the mask, filled with love and the willingness to light the lives of all those around him. The man I flirted with outrageously; the man my soul married.

Three of our five years together sailing became an unbearable struggle, an up and down roller coaster filled with beauty and wonder, and anger and insults. Wayne desperately trying to hang onto the spiritual world that had always fit so neatly in his pocket and I, desperate to build a trust with my feelings, to trust that they had a basis deeper than any I could have ever dreamed. We went on with our insults and barbs interspersed with all the good times, and there were so many. How could there not be. We were living in that high frequency world of beauty and grace only nature can create, getting closer and closer to this woman neither of us had ever bothered to understand before; rolling around the bunk, making love to the rhythm of Her waves, swimming with rays, flirting with squid, challenging the dolphins to play. It's not always easy breaking through the old stone tablets, but if you're going to try, sailing on the archetypal waters of the Great Mother is a great way to go!

I'm not sure there are enough adjectives in our language to accurately describe the years of sailing upon the waters of our oceans, first with Wayne on Merlin then alone on my boat, Ko Le'a, let alone try to describe life on a boat. A sailboat takes on its own unique personality under sail. Everything it does is in harmony with all around it; they don't plough through the waters, they gracefully lift their bow to the wave, let it pass under them, then move gracefully on their way. They play with the dolphins that come to surf their wakes, surrender their sheets to a gust of wind, and if they're lucky enough to have a captain who knows what he's doing, they'll back their sails and head into the winds of a storm for as long as is needed.

But for Wayne and me every day was a miracle. When it's your watch, you learn to live with a heightened sense of excitement and tension, then learn how to sleep with the same excitement and tension. Making meals while dancing the sailor's two step; drinking early morning coffee while watching a whale on your stern, or dolphins jump in your wake and watching every sunrise and sunset appear with their own unique signature, becomes your daily routine. Day after day, night after night, there's a sense you can't shake of living within the breath of something ageless, within the nation of ancientness, still and quiet, alive and moving, ever flowing back and forth within its own womb. When you are new to it, there is a constant ghostly sense of being watched through the eyes of one who has been here forever, following you and everything you do; and in your head, your shoulders, your belly is a strong sense of the Feminine, both vulnerable and fearsome; spilling out from the ocean to the land. At some point, you begin to get it–

41

although this has often been referred to a man's world, the truth is, it's very much a woman's; not recognizing that, or denying it, says a lot about our ability to simply see what is, you're not just living side by side with nature, you are living in her house, her nation; you are the guest and English is the 2$^{nd}$ language. Without realizing it, I was not just beginning to learn/speak my Mother Tongue; I was beginning to think in this language. One night while on watch, I could hear the sound of breath all around me and I knew we had sailed into a pod of dolphins or whales and as they moved along side of us, the moon was rising full, red, and awesome. Through the entire watch, I felt as though I was a stranger who had just stepped into a wet and wild world that would change everything I had ever known. I thought back to a couple Wayne and I met with in Arizona who had spent a year sailing in the Caribbean. We wanted to pick their brains about the experience. His most memorable comment was that the ocean was just another desert, a vast, deserted, rambling nothingness. While Wayne (and apparently himself) felt this was an epiphany, it left me wondering if he had, indeed, actually been on the ocean.

Wayne turned out to be an amazingly gifted sailor. He could read a chart and pick out all the dents and curves within it as though he was reading an architectural plan. For the most part, reading an unfamiliar coast line thru the chart was a mystery to me. He seemed to intuit every nuance and need of the boat like I could intuit the presence of a spirit. Once, in the Bahamas we had some people on board who had come to take a spiritual course I was giving at the time and we got stuck on a shoal not far from another boat that was stuck. He raised the sail full blast and tightened it as much as possible and the wind veered us around until the hull was free and we sailed out. We were all yelling at the top of our lungs, happy to be free and life seemed to be so good at that moment.

Our journey thru the Caribbean was one wonder after another, filled with strange cultural myths, flowers and foliage that knew no boundaries; of woven baskets & birds from families with names made up of too many vowels, n's and g's all strung together, of swimming thru schools of Parrot fish that looked like children's art and literally walking on water when we saw a school of barracuda. Although, on the island of St. Bart's, I was talking to a gal from another boat who told of an incredible incident with her nephew. They had gone snorkeling and a school of barracuda came by, circled her nephew then surrounded him. All at once they turned heads up in the water and just hung there, pressing near to him, and stayed that way for what seemed an eternity to her, but was probably only seconds. Then they all swam off. She had no idea what to make of it, but it was one of those moments in life when you are suspended between utter fear and complete and utter awe. I love those moments!

We sailed through the lush abundance of the volcanic islands of Martinique, St. Martens, which bore fruits and vegetables we'd never seen before and made me realize that this planet was and still is the Garden of Eden. In the Los Roces an Osprey came to sit on our stern and eat his fish. It came for 3 days after, each time leaving us gifts of stones, shells, ocean debris. The island of Saba loomed like the original lost island of pirate novels, rising out of nowhere in the middle of the ocean with steep vertical cliffs. There was no safe harbor, but we dropped anchor and went ashore anyway. How could you not? How many magnificent waterfalls–one side hot & steamy from volcano, the other ice cold–we learned about sisal, which can be used for twine, mats, ropes, and even clothing; and ate the jelly inside the coconut, which I had no idea was there.

On Carriacou we got to know the Islanders who were building boats; by hand with hand tools! They were so remarkable! We were lucky enough to be there during one of their biggest race weekends. This tiny island is surrounded by reefs with only a few ways to get thru and it was in the most reef strewn part of the island that they held their race. That morning we met with a Captain we had gotten to know at the local hang out everyone gathered before the race. There was whiskey, pot, and jibes aplenty between all the contestants and both Wayne and I were afraid they were too drunk or stoned to go thru with it. But race they did, in and out of the reefs and shallow water, into the deep blue and around the island, then back in again through the reef strewn passages, all under sail–none of the boats had engines. We began to recognize the sophisticated knowledge the islanders had that made it so easy to live so closely with nature, but most of all, we realized how much of that knowledge we'd lost thinking it unnecessary, that we'd always be able to get what we need from the store and technology.

And the wild, Saturday night Jump-ups with their steel drums, guitars, flutes, even pots and pans; everyone dancing in the street, lost in the music, going from partner to partner. Music was in the air, the very essence of the islands, in fact you could say that music was their 1st language. In the mornings, some Rasta would be running down the street, singing at the top of his lungs a song only the island knew. And the women; they never walk, they sway, hum and saunter, balancing baskets of fruit on their heads, moving back and forth from tiny little huts set back in a rain forest. On many of the islands the beaches were filled, not with tourists, but with children running bare foot in among the reefs and the nets being mended, in among the pirogues, cayucas, the torn or patched sails being mended.

We met other sailors and shared stories of how paralyzed we felt the first time we ate breadfruit or poi and realized we had to eat with our fingers. We watched how their faces lit up when speaking about the first time they attended a cava-cava ceremony, and heard the sound of the 'pounding of the stones', with moonlight streaming across the water, across the feast and faces.

"You'll think me a bloke, but it was the first time I have ever worn a wreath of yellow ginger on my head…" one sailor said, "funny, it's something I will cherish always."

Jane, his wife made a comment I'll never forget.

"It's all so overwhelmingly sensual, life just becomes sensual," she said. "Makes you feel your own womanhood, like a mirror reflecting back to you your own wild, untamed beauty. There you are, some witchy wild haired midwife playing with the wind as it crawls all over your body, laughing at the river as it rises to threaten your garden. I love it."

But most of all, it was every moment, each incident that occurred that was trying–succeeding–to bring me back into balance. One such incident just happens to be a great fish story. Actually, I hated killing fish, I loved to eat it, but hated sticking the knife in. Once Wayne hauled in a huge, glittering Mahi Mahi. It was flopping and whoomphing all over the deck and the hatch to the aft cabin was open, it moved so fast, it nearly landed in our bunk! Finally, he jumped on it, and shouted

"Quick, get the knife and stab it behind the eyes."

I was so stunned; it took me forever to do it. But he loved to fish. There were days when he'd just toss the line over board, haul in fish, pull it off the hook, toss it back, then do the same thing over and over. Actually, he could practically whistle a fish on board, he was a natural born hunter.

Then, we came into a time, week after week when he couldn't catch anything. Time after time, day after day, nothing; absolutely no fish to be had. Finally I went up to the bow, sat there for a while, watching Merlin slice through the water and just got quiet. Under sail, there's this natural, yet unnatural sense of quiet on the bow that can't really be explained. All this action happening at once, the winds breathe out loud making bulging pockets of the sail, your boat slices through the parting waters that flow to each side; rainbows dust the bow and the world explodes into a moving, measured beat of eternity. Yet nothing seems disturbed, as though every particle in motion is so finely tuned, so symphonic, that everything seems to happen harmoniously. It's one of my favorite places. I closed my eyes and asked a question.

"I know something's going on, what is it? Why haven't we caught any fish?" No one was there, I was just asking that gut presence inside; that motionless motion going on. Very clear and unmistakable, a voice answered.

"Do not hoard, you need only one fish for your supper. You'll always have it. Honor it, see it, know it, and give it thanks. It is a gift!"

It spoke of honor between us and kill; generations of trust between all living things, of simple needs fulfilled that somehow fulfills the needs of all, of an abundant ripple of service spiraling outward into a greater circle until the circle grows and grows and grows. Service. We are all in service to each other.

I didn't question this or its source. It was like the certainty of dreams and, like a catalyst, it sent pictures running through my head with ideas that I have always known, but never knew I knew—does that make sense? With that simple admonition, I realized that everything and everyone of us on earth is in service to each other, that is our bond, our family legacy to each other; that it wasn't so much about being or not being a vegetarian, but more about how we honor the service to each other. Instinctively, I understood the real reason why we bless our food and how out of balance we were with that bond. How everything, fish, cow, pig, lettuce & cucumber, and mankind, each deserves to be seen, to be acknowledged, to be thanked for the service we give one another.

Later that afternoon we caught a tuna. Determined to trust, I went up to it, opened my hands and gave thanks. Inexplicably, enigmatically, a substance seemed to escape from the body of that tuna, leaving me stunned. I knew it was the spirit, the soul of that fish. I was amazed at the clarity that had manifested right in front of my eyes. I didn't tell Wayne about it, we had already had some disagreements about what I was experiencing and how he experienced our new world of wonder; I knew I had to keep this safe within me or risk losing it to another argument. Every time afterwards, however, whenever we fished, we caught a tuna. Each time I quietly thanked the tuna–not God for giving it to me–but the tuna itself. It felt right to give thanks to whom thanks was due.

# Chapter 6–Dominique

Sometimes the enormous joy we had was just simply sitting at anchor, at night, watching the stars and feeling the movement of our boat rocking softly, gracefully, with the current. We were in a tiny little cove at Martinique with a dear friend, Penny, who had flown over to join us and an amazing evening occurred. We were on the stern talking softly about the magic in our lives, high as a kite on the beauty of it all.

Penny was extraordinary, she could shift your energy just by touching you; one time after giving Wayne a massage, he started laughing and crying at the same time and couldn't stop, he was so open and vulnerable at that time, as though all the love in the world had poured into him. She was an amazing healer; and a big believer in her alien friends. Maybe because of her strength in that belief, she helped me to see the glowing orbs that quite often surrounded her.

But back to that evening, we suddenly noticed that all around the cove were these tiny sparkling lights moving and jumping about. She laughed and suggested that we invite them onto the boat. They began to move forward, towards us as though taking us up on the offer; to this day I have no idea what they were, but it was an amazing sight to watch their display as they twinkled and inched towards the boat. Just as they were about to touch Merlin, they stopped and began to retreat. Penny and I began laughing like two novice witches playing with fire– both alarmed and amazed at the same time. Life had most definitely turned from black and white to blinding

Technicolor yet once again! Penny became an integral piece of my life, a lifetime friend and sister. She was going to play an enormous role in my life of miracles.

Not all the Islanders were happy to see us. On St. Lucia, home of the famous Pitons, there were parts of the island that seemed almost off limits to us with white skin. There were so many angry and bewildered people there who felt betrayed somehow, that the promise given by foreign developers of money and riches had never meant to include them. While asking around one day, we found out about a developer's plan to build a revolving restaurant on top of the Pitons. How long can we go through life blind, unable to see the incredible gifts Mother Earth gives us for free? If I could find that point that turns one's back on the Lord of Money and ignites our hearts on fire with the beauty of our planet, I think I would spend my life spreading it all over the planet. It was then that I began to feel a burning outrage that began to boil inside.

It was on the island of Dominique that I began to have a series of dreams that spilled over to daylight. Dominique is so wild, so untamed you have to fight your way through a jungle of wild ginger, frangipani; trees I swear were sculpted by some ancient, green forest artist. It was there that the waterfalls boiled hot and cold simultaneously from the volcano and the icy mountain streams. We had met a shy, chubby village girl named Senta who took us for a hike through her backyard rain forest. She loved Wayne, kept clinging to his hand and he giggled like a young boy. She took us to some quiet, out of the way sulfur pools, grottoes and caves. It's such an extraordinary, lush, verdant island; I could only think of it as a woman spirit manifest as an island mountain, the jungle streaming down her back like long tangled hair of jade, shades of every color green you could imagine. The over-abundant flowers were her jewels and the heavy scent of lush mixture her perfume.

One hot afternoon when Wayne was sleeping, I jumped in the crystal blue waters around our boat just to float on my back and cool down. It was a way I found to meditate, just float on my back for what seemed like hours and let my mind dissolve to nothingness. Looking up, I saw what felt like her rain forest mountains looking down at me with a stern stubborn stare. I couldn't remember inviting this, but there it was. The waters seemed to change suddenly, or maybe I changed, but they felt healing somehow. Some healing force going on. It was the first time I felt such a strong healing force in the waters. That night I had the strangest dream...

A woman took me deep inside the rain forest and began to slowly change, back and forth, from energy to form, from nothing to woman, always watching my reaction each time she altered her shape. Then she pointed at the huts I had seen earlier that day, they appeared then disappeared, then reappeared again, back and forth, dissolving into the rain forest, into the bamboo, the trees and fronds, then transformed back again into huts. Through it all she never spoke, just kept looking at me with the same sense of sternness I had felt while in the water. She then took me to bathe in a shower of mountain water but I couldn't feel the wetness, instead it seemed to crawl inside my skin, cleansing from the inside out, as though everything was happening from the inside-out. The same thing happened when she took me to dry, from the air and sun, inside out, inside out. Something so familiar flashed through my memory, it felt alive, but went too fast I couldn't hold on to it. She kept looking at me as if to say 'you understand, understand, understand'. I did, but I didn't, what was it that had flashed through my thoughts so quickly?

I talked to Wayne about it the next morning, over a breakfast of mangoes, papaya, cornmeal pancakes and a sunrise that mixed all those colors into one.

"You know, I'm beginning to feel dogged, afraid to step on a bug for fear you'll have some weird damn dream about it. Can we just get thru the day?" was all he said.

When it came to defense, we were both drama queens. We had just 'gotten through the day' for the last two weeks, climbing mountains, playing guitars with reggae masters, entangled in each other's arms in some hot sultry sulfur pool. But we could still display our little scenes.

"I've got to get to the market today, want to come? I replied.

It was an empty gesture; I knew he didn't because he was going spear fishing with Senta's brother. I just wanted to diffuse the tension. I didn't even need to go to the market, just felt a need to wander among the open stalls of tomatoes, chickens, calaloo and calabash, and haggle with my favorite lady. Which was everyone who had a stall.

Pictures from my dream met me at each stall, while the words 'understand, understand' were breathing in and out all around me. I'd ask 'how much is the fish today' and she'd answer with a scene from the river where women washed clothes and husbands fished, fish fished, currents washed away the debris, and sunlight dove down as far as it could to wake the anemone on coral. Some fat tummyed little boy would come up to gawk at me and I'd see his mother humming him to sleep in a hammock strung from tree to tree. I began to physically grasp that flash of insight I couldn't hold onto earlier, that we're really born from this beautiful mixture of the essence of Nature and essence of illusion, flowing in and out of each other, in and out of a mystery womb that knows no boundaries between worth or not, animal or human, and every piece of land within the arms of Mother Ocean were just tiny little islands whether you called it America, Europe, or Dominique. And we're all connected through this womb, this spiritual planet we live on, connected, everything is connected.

I walked away listening to something inside shouting 'Don't lose the feeling! Come closer...' It was the feeling one gets, if they're lucky, on a deserted beach in Santa Barbara, or a hilltop at sunset overlooking a vast stretch of verdant valleys, or at the birth of a new babe.

Maybe luck has nothing to do with it. Maybe it's an inner knowing we all too often allow to be severed. I've just never known anyone to get it watching TV, especially the news, unless your newscaster happens to be the voice of Nature, or one of her emissaries. I wanted so bad to talk to Wayne about it all, to share my feelings.

That evening we went to our favorite restaurant in town, a local bar that served the best seafood soup this side of Venus.

"Wayne, I think there's a reason this ancient idea of a Goddess, like Mother Earth, Mother Nature, Sister Ocean has never left us. I think we women are more tied to her than we want to believe and that somehow, her life story is intertwined with women all through the ages."

"Why just women? What's up with that?" He challenged.

"I don't know, maybe we're just more in tune with her. I keep getting a rush of pictures like Earth is Eden. Or Eden is a state of mind. Maybe we lost it when we severed our link to the Mother. Maybe Eve's tale was just a metaphor explain how closely linked women are to the earth and all creatures; or about what would happen if Women gave up that link, maybe we're living that curse now". I fell over this little speech like I was tumbling down a waterfall; it all came so quick, fast as the falling waters.

"Like what? What exactly, in all this 'extrapolation,'" he said, using his finger tips to quote "has happened?"

"A spiritual caste system..." I screamed, unable to stop myself. "...between Earth and Heaven, man, women and beast, holy and lowly, us and them. All delivered with a promise to be saved if only we believed, adhered to that caste system."

I sounded so blasted self-righteous but I couldn't stop myself. And neither could Wayne, although I'm sure he wanted to. Both of us just kept puking it all up.

"I don't want to hear this!" he pleaded. "Every day you sound more and more like a loud-mouthed Feminist. You're becoming just like them; you never followed the crowd before, what's going on?"

"You finished?" The dark-haired waitress came up so quickly we both jumped.

"No. Not at all. Can we get some more hot rolls?" They were the best. The anger that came over me just didn't fit with the candlelight or the soft rain falling down all around this little jungle bar. A place better suited to the blending of romantics and visionaries than the bitter adversaries we were becoming. I barfed up yet another answer I wished I'd had time to edit.

"Oh, I see. Tell me, under which doctrine does one finally 'think for themselves'? Yours? Christian, Jew, Atheist? Democrat, liberal, conservative? The doctrine of all those past and present Clergy who put their own territorial piss on all biblical teachings like some kind of male bond with a male God? Well, here's the thing, women had a strong bond to the Mother and the severance of that bond has left us with a history of fires still needing to be put out; environmentally, politically, economically, we don't have the loud-mouth-voice of the Mother anymore and it's killing us!"

It was getting loud and I had no idea where I was going with this thought, but it felt as though I had grasped a string connecting the dots to what was I felt was out of kilter–out of balance–between us, Earth and all her inhabitants. At that moment, however, it served only to dig the trench deeper between Wayne and I, and yet, it could have done just the opposite; it could have brought us closer. I rallied at his inability to understand me, he called me a Feminist, but here's the funny thing. At times I even found myself asking him for money, or permission to go dancing (he hated dancing). Eleven years as an independent business woman, and still I slipped in and out of some wifey role while asserting some deep Mother instinct wisdom. No wonder we got so confused, moving back and forth between revelations that freed us and old rituals that sunk us–the ones lurking in the back streets of our unconscious, paternal minds. I always regretted lashing out the way I did at that time; it seemed so petty and yet I could hardly stop it. Would it have been more of a service would I have simply stated my views calmly with compassion? That was a lesson I needed to learn in my life.

We ended up slapping each other around quite a bit, emotionally, verbally, then finally physically. Slapping around never ends, until it ends, entirely. On and on it went, until the black, ugly death of our relationship; a death without honor that would haunt me for years. The next time you ask someone what it was like sailing through the islands, watch their eyes; there may be a story in there your question rattled.

Sometimes our differences turned into a bed of roses; times when his enormous ability to guide Merlin through the reefs, in between giant cavernous cliffs to some secret, hidden anchorage and my sense of the mystical, wonder and awe worked for us, not against us. At those times, like clawing our way through the rock and reef strewn waters that surround the island of Eleuthera, I was in awe of him; then when we had to break a lock to get thru the hatch of a beached boat and somehow I just knew the correct sequence of numbers we needed, he was in awe of me. Those times, and there were many, we worked together like a fine tuned off-world instrument and we both shared hope that we could make it.

Once, in St. Thomas, we both experienced that scary world of Sacred Humor. It used to be, when I was younger, the word Sacred would instill a sense of somber stillness, the color of black robes and 3 tiny candles left burning on the altar of some tiny alcove lit from the dawn colored rays of stained glass. But this time I learned of the Sacred color of Humor, like the iridescent colors that form on the bubbles a child blows from a bubble bottle, or the iridescence that forms on ice crystals in the winter; Sacred humor is hilariously iridescent. I was in the throes of that high vibration in which everything comes your way so easily all you can do is giggle. Wayne needed an extra hose for some chore he was doing, it took exactly 3 minutes for me to walk out on the dock and find one that had been abandoned; he needed some plumbing fixtures, I went to introduce myself to some people who had just come in and they just happened to be tossing out a basket of plumbing fixtures; exactly what he needed. This went on for the entire morning when Wayne suggested that perhaps now would be a great time to find the claw foot anchor he had been searching for, with no success, for months.

"Let's go out and find one!" I said, laughing at how simple it would now be.

We rented a car and drove to the nearest boat hardware store and found nothing in the way of claw foot anchors–all sold out they said. After two or three more misses, we decided to drive over to the other side of the island where it wasn't so populated by us boaters. We spotted a combination diner, hardware & all-purpose store in a tiny village and decided to stop for a bite to eat. We started talking to the owner, an Islander who had sailed around the islands himself. While sharing stories and nightmares, Wayne suddenly asked

"You don't perhaps have a claw foot storm anchor hanging around, do you?"

"Yeah, got one in the back. You want to see it?" the man said.

We were both amazed; pleased, and baffled at the same time. I started to smile. He brought it out, uncovered it and there sat exactly what Wayne had been looking for.

"How much do you want for it?" Wayne asked.

"Oh. It's not for sale! Wouldn't want to part with it. Sorry." It wasn't the reply we expected!

I couldn't begin to tell you the disbelief that rung my bell at his statement, the almost pure incredulity that marked Wayne's face–a "This can't be happening" look was emanating all over his body. Mine too, it was downright embarrassing. What just happened to my "think it, find it" experiences?

We left shortly after that and remained silent in the car for almost the entire trip back to the docks. It wasn't until that evening that I remembered my statement to him just before we had left earlier that morning: "Let's go find one!" We did. We got exactly what we had set out to do. Sacred Humor, it takes a while to get used to, but it's really funny once you get the hang of it.

# Chapter 7—Antigua, Los Roces, ABC Islands

It was in Antigua when Wayne decided to try his–ours, actually–hand at racing. Antigua has a huge 2- or 3-week celebration (if you can string it out that long, which most sailors manage to do) surrounding their race week. Sailors from all over the world come to compete. What were we thinking? Wayne invited some buddies from Flagstaff to come, bring their wives, and spend the month with us. One of them, Don, was a seasoned racer and with his help, we felt we had a great chance to make a name for ourselves. We did, but not the name we wanted. Merlin, for all her red sails, black masts, teak decks was a wide, comfortable live-aboard, that tended to, due to her wide body, sail sideways when faced with heavy winds. Definitely not a racer! But we entered anyway and spent many a night listening to Don explain the finer points of getting off the starting line first and rounding the racing buoy with grace and speed. I'm not sure, but I think we got off the starting line last, or pretty close to last; we couldn't manage to get her turned around quickly enough and miss all the other boats moving every which way around us. We did get off, however, and pulled the sails in as tightly as we could to make the most headway we could. Several crashes below deck sent me reeling as fast as I could where I soon discovered that with all the "race handling" we had done, it wasn't enough–things were still flying around; the pantry door flew open and food was everywhere, someone had left their goodies in the guest head unchecked, the music tapes (still in use then) managed to get free from where I had stored them. I shouted–Stop, Stop,–but of course no one paid attention; I turned out to be a lousy sailor. I went back up and glared menacingly at everyone top deck, I didn't like sailing on my side and felt almost certain Merlin didn't either–our boat was straining to make any headway and all we managed to do was get further and further behind. At one point an hour or so into the race, we noticed a boat ahead of us appear from what seemed nowhere; it appeared to be picking up the racing buoys.

Wayne got on the race radio channel to hear what was going on, what we all heard was:

Boat in sight: "does anyone know about that boat with the red sails?"

Committee: "does it have a racing number?"

Pause. Boat in sight: "Actually, it does! How strange."

Committee: "You'll have to wait until it passes the buoys before picking them up then."

Pause. Boat in sight: "Oh brother."

We did make it to the final buoy and rounded it before dark. There was no one there to greet us or clap for us, however, and to be honest, that was probably due to the fact that we rounded the buoy going the wrong way. We didn't even make it into the list of those who finished, however badly. I think that everyone on board believed our failure was my fault–I should never have screamed Stop, and glared at everyone like a withering banshee. I tend to agree with them. It was probably one of my least favorite incidences of my entire lifetime! But there you are. Some people actually had the audacity to ask us the next day if we were the ones in the boat with the red sails. There is no limit to how rude people can be sometimes. One very nice man, however, perhaps while under the influence of a few too many did say he was sorry.

"Honestly, I think they really do need a special category for live-aboard boats, don't you?" he said.

We just nodded and bought him another drink.

More and more the shift in perspective, seeing the world through the eyes of a Woman, thinking in the language of the Mother, began to color my perspective and increase the distance between Wayne and me. We were in the chain of tiny islands called Los Roces, on the outskirts of Venezuela when I realized that the change was becoming more imminent. We were sailing with another couple, they had a Trimaran and could easily skim across the rocks, and we'd anchor together in the most incredible settings of reef, crystal clear waters, tiny palm splayed islets and sunrises and sunsets you get once a year on a calendar depicting nature at her best. We snorkeled among schools of enormous iridescent tri-colored parrot fish and graceful blue-black manta rays; every day Susan would dive down deeper than either Wayne or George could and bring up hordes of lobster and conch. Every morning, every evening we would feast on lobster omelets, conch fritters or steaks; it was gluttonous pleasure in every way you could imagine.

It was exactly this feeling that re-awakened what I had been taught before, with the tuna. My joy at this easy feast began to weaken as my bond with my surroundings began to assert itself. It reached its peak one day while

Wayne was preparing a conch for dinner. There is only one way to do this–you have to tear it, muscle by muscle, sinew by sinew away from its shell. I was sitting next to him on the forward deck looking out over that pre-sunset indigo blue that colors the formerly clear bright sky. I turned my head at the exact moment the conch turned its head and looked me right in the eye. I can only tell you that it had to be that deep, penetrating woman-to-nature-creature-bond that told me that we had made contact, and the contact was painful; unbearably painful. We had forgotten to honor, give thanks, communicate to the creature that would serve as our next meal–to all the creatures who had served at our pleasure. I could no longer do it, could no longer take pride in catching conch and lobster for breakfast, lunch and dinner. Wayne thought I was crazy, yet again.

We left Los Roces and Venezuela and headed for the ABC islands; Bonaire, Curacao and Aruba. We were picking up Steve, my old buddy, in Bonaire. I loved that island, the island of Flamingos and tiny little sea horses, an overabundance of reefs to snorkel thru and beautiful island people to mingle with. Bonaire had one large crescent shaped anchorage close to the shore that was incredibly peaceful, especially at night with the lights from the town mingling with starlight and soft lapping waters. There was just one problem, it was windward. We became friends with a young couple aboard a boat called Condi, who sailed from Africa and loved to drink beer and tell rugby stories. In the middle of one seemingly peaceful night, we woke to screaming and yelling from all the boats round us; the dreaded winds had come in and we were all being pushed toward shore. I'm not sure how we did it, but between one breath and another, we pulled up one anchor and just cut the line on the other then pulled and yanked Merlin around like a horse that had gone out of control and fought our way out to safety in the open waters. When we could breathe again, we got on the radio and called around for our friends, we couldn't see them anywhere. It was hours later when we got the call from another boat that they weren't so lucky, they'd been pushed ashore and were beached. I'm not sure there is anything more painful than to see a sailboat lying on her side, hull exposed, completely vulnerable to an environment alien to everything she was made for.

This is where I learned to love the islanders of Bonaire; the next morning we went to see Nan, Patrick and Condi and offer some assistance but there they were being hauled up onto a makeshift cradle in the middle of someone's yard, safe and sound and ready for repair! I was so glad for them, they'd been offered a room in their host's house, and all the help they needed. We on the other hand, decided to pull into the safety of the boat docks on the lee side of the anchorage. Bonaire was good for us all! We celebrated my birthday one night with an African dish called Baboulli that Nan made–a meat dish with chutney, nuts, jam and potatoes–spent days helping with Condi, chasing after pink flamingos, wandering the streets and drinking Dutch ale at every waterfront café we could. But soon, it was time to move on.

The day Wayne, Steve and I, along with our two boat cats, Smorgasbord-Morgie and Lanceless (he was originally called Lancelot, but got cut) decided to leave for

Curacao we headed out to open waters and sighted a water spout off our port side. In all honesty, we watched it move and jump for a full 10 minutes before we hightailed it back in to port. I didn't care that most of our comrades were cat-calling and jeering on the radio, some experiences you just don't want to run into eyes wide open. We left the following day–it was beautiful and clear.

We pulled into Curacao among the most amazing antiquity; Dutch colonial homes and buildings surrounded the anchorage, cobblestone streets and people who seemed as though they have lived there for eternity. Although I loved it, I had the strangest sense of my equilibrium being off. We spent a couple of weeks there and decided it was time to head out to Aruba to gas up for the next leg. We never even got off the boat on Aruba; we all had the sense needing to leave. Some islands leave you feeling that way, I have no idea why. We fueled up and set out for the Bay Islands of Honduras, Guanaja, Cayos Cochinos, Utila and Roatan.

# Chapter 8–The Jaws and the Beauty of a Storm

We'd been sailing for about 2 and 1/2 years by now, but still, every time you trek out into open sea it's like the very first time; thrilling, peaceful, unnerving, alien yet comfortable and always the wild vastness of it amazes you. Will the Dolphins or the pilot whales come to play, how long before you see another boat or will it just be you alone on that immense, ever changing living wet highway? How long before you start to breathe again with the rhythm of the waves, harness the winds, work with the swells in balance, in harmony?   You watch your bow slicing thru the virgin waters, your wake following behind and you're not sure you're a child looking at the footsteps in new fallen snow, or an adult facing a brave new world. Wayne hauled out the fishing rod, Steve learned to puke on the lee side and I did everything I could to tune back in to that She-speak, water-speak, living pulse of Mother Ocean.

It was about two days out when the storm hit. Black. Ugly. Unbelievably powerful. The winds tore at our face, neck and shoulders; all sense of where we were, any control we felt just disappeared. All we could think about was survival; getting the sales down, reducing speed, it was as though we had sailed right into a maelstrom. Steve and Wayne crawled forward to bring down the jib, but the mechanism froze halfway down. They tied it as best they could but for seven days Merlin shook as though we were driving down the highway with a flat tire. That's how long it lasted, seven days, with winds shrieking in our ears, waves as high as a mountain looming over the stern, picking Merlin up and slamming her back down. I tried to stow anything that was loose into our bunk when I wasn't slammed into the bulkheads, bruise after bruise as black and blue as the sky. The thunderous sky looked as though it was forming massive fists that seemed to slam into the water and cause more waves to rile upwards in retaliation.

Day and night, it never stopped, the winds would peak to 50 knots, and you'd think it was ending when they dropped to 30 or so...but no, they were just taking a break. Every night we backed Merlin into the winds and tried to rest–it's almost impossible to do–and tried to sail under triple reef during the day, but it was no good; all we did was buck the monstrous winds, and slam dance against the seas–Mother Ocean had gone crazy, she was green and roiling, angry and lashing out at everything in her path. Every breath, every step–even trying to rest or eat–was an effort you weren't sure you could continue, but you had to, there was no stopping it, no 7-11 to run into to get out of the storm for a bit; no matter how much you wanted to shout–just stop for a minute–you knew there was nothing you could do but continue on–never knowing its name, where did it come from, will it ever end–you just continue on. Three days, four days, five, six, seven; we were exhausted, broken and depressed, our fingers black and blue from hanging on.

We finally just lay backed into the winds hoping it would soon end. One day I saw Morgie darting across the deck, trying to get below when a wave hit and I was sure she went overboard. I became as angry as the Ocean, the winds, the sky. I balled up my fists and lashed out at God,

67

the heavens, everything I could think of–I didn't lash out at the Goddess, only because I didn't think of her, had I she too would have faced my bitter tongue and rage. I was almost sure Morgie was pregnant, from a stray cat in Bonaire; I just couldn't believe I had lost her–lost her to this ugly, maniacal ocean. I just couldn't believe it.

Day seven the winds abated a bit, I came topside and looked at the mountain of water coming down on our stern, then grabbed the nearest stay and for the first time, just looked at everything around me–the war zone, the waves still crashing into each other, the blackened bruised sky, Merlin pitching around like a drunk–I looked and watched and suddenly I could not believe how awesome, how unbelievably beautiful it all was. That's all I could think, that it was the most incredible, unleashed power of beauty-horror I had ever seen. At that moment, something so profound shifted inside that I knew I would be forever grateful for seven frightening days witnessing the power and fury of my Mother Ocean. Later that day, Ms. Smorgasbord-Morgie came out from hiding to see what was happening. Oh, I was so happy.

Two days later we spotted Guanaja off in the distance. Later that evening we pulled into empty calm lagoon, anchored, and I was immediately mesmerized. It was magical. Immediately I knew I would grow to love this tiny little haven. On the left was the mountainous verdant green island rising up, dipping into valleys then rising again, on the right was the village itself built on wood planks out over the water, attached to the main island by a tiny causeway. Apparently, the island had enormous mosquitoes and the villagers had decided it was inhabitable–there be monsters on that isle!

It's funny how each island imprints itself into a kaleidoscope of living memories packed with colors, smells, the sounds of laughter and music; I close my eyes to remember Guanaja and see shades of blue and shadows and damp wood, moss greens and the laughter of two young boys rowing out to our boat introducing themselves as brothers though one was a beautiful shade of black and the other as blonde as I was; walking on wood planks with water lapping below us.

All of the out-islands were the descendants of English pirates who had settled these out-islands years and years ago, sharp lapis blue eyes, dark hair and crème colored skin; or the descendants of slaves who had been brought in all those years ago. But if there was a class structure, no one seemed to know it, they worked, laughed, sang, and played music together like one huge family.

When I think back to Utila I see golds and soft greens, reefs & driftwood strewn beaches, but most of all I remember the couple we became friends with, he of the pirates and she of the mainland, he speaking English, she Spanish and neither spoke each other's language–or so they said–and their little boy translated for each of them. I don't know, that's what they said anyway! Utila was so small you could walk it in an hour and a half; with no electricity except for one generator at the tiny grocery store in the middle of the town. Every day the whole island would gather at the store to talk-talk and buy what was needed for the evening meal–an onion or potatoes, some flower maybe for tortillas, rice for the fish stew. I loved this idea, it was so perfect and somehow, just harmonious. We went back and forth between Guanaja and Utila for a couple of months and found it so hard to leave. For all that time, we were the only boat at either island. Between them both, my world just sank into this tiny-soft-pillow-warm-tender-archipelago of island days with smiles and hugs, fried fish and warm tortillas.

Roatan brought with it some different memories; it was so much bigger, we all felt as though we had left small town planet Earth and moved to the big city. It was a bit unsettling at first, although our first anchorage was a small cove, I couldn't help but think that it has safely hid many a pirate in the day. We spent a few solitary nights there before moving into the big city. We found an anchorage outside of what was hailed as a Yacht Club–a tiny bar to be more precise where sailors from all over had gathered throughout all time. We rowed over, tied up, went inside and ordered a beer. Here, I was to have one of the strangest experiences–you couldn't call it spiritual, yet it left an impression on my spirit so heavy I will never forget it. They had television–which we had not seen for over 3 years. I got a beer and sat down to watch.

The President of the US was speaking, George Bush, Sr., giving his State of the Union Address. Other than my time in Texas and knowing him then as a politician on the move, I had no impression of him as the leader of the United States. Watching him speak, however, I began to get sick to my stomach, so much so, that I had to leave and found myself heaving in the bathroom. I kept thinking at the time, 'this is a soap opera, something is wrong'. I have to stress here that I had no particular views of him at the time; I knew it was not him that was causing the illness. I thought about it for days afterwards wondering what had happened–something was wrong! Then it hit me, and when it did it was like a bolt of lightning. We had been unplugged for nearly three year, living day to day in this incredible world of nature and nature's children, in beauty and wonder. Television had intruded and on a deeper level somehow, I knew that what I was watching was an illusion, it wasn't real and my body reacted on a cellular level–like a toxin that had just been injected out of the blue–I reacted violently; I am not, nor have ever been a purist, putting only the most pure foods into my system, never drinking, never smoking, but at that moment I felt as tho I had been a purist. Steve and I talked about later that evening; he didn't laugh or question my sanity, gratefully. But he did mention reading a couple of articles on the effects of the negative vibrations that TV induced. I have never forgotten this lesson; to this day I can feel the toxic intrusion of television and the agenda of those delivering their message.

Vincent, a descendant of one of the original English pirates on Roatan, befriended us and we became great buddies. We spent a lot of time walking the island, meeting his friends and family, playing music, and generally learning how life was celebrated on Roatan. The reefs surrounding Roatan were lush with fish and vegetation–it was great snorkeling. One day while at one of the family warehouses where Vincent worked, we were shown an enormous storage unit filled with a hoard of lobster.

"We never eat it," he quipped, "it's all set to ship to your States."

Wayne was amazed, as was Steve; I was simply bewildered. It seemed so strange that being so obviously abundant, it would not have been one of their staples. There was a story here.

"It's not that abundant, really, not any more at least, all fished out. We have to hire the mainland Mayans to come in and dive out on the out-reefs, only place that's abundant now. Deep out there, too deep to make much more than a couple of dives, but they do it anyway, and die. Many of them die, but it's good pay! They want it."

It was a moving story; even Wayne was moved. I learned a lot that day; things like how important it is to know where your luxuries come from–lobster whenever we want? Is this always a good idea? How are people's lives affected by our lack of knowledge? How much pain do we cause with our thirst for luxury?

We spent a couple of months sailing around the Bay Islands, snorkeling, diving, always on the look-out for whale sharks, never seeing them; flying over the mountains of Honduras in a bush plane with a pilot from Cayos Cochinos. Meeting people we loved and hung out with, then always the inevitable–saying goodbye. It was time for us to move on to Belize and Guatemala; we were planning on staying in that area for quite a while.

# Chapter 9–Belize and Guatemala; the End of a Relationship

The trip over was uneventful, a few rough seas, high winds, but nothing like the storm we had encountered. Steve got over his sea sickness and took a few shifts of his own giving Wayne and I a chance for some much-needed alone time.

No matter how many times you have watched a sunset at sea, the one you are watching right now is always the first! Maybe it's being alone on the ocean, feeling the truth of being one small particle of the enormous beauty of our planet, maybe its feeling as though, at any moment during this spectacular scene, sunset or sunrise, every element or particle that makes up the whole will come sliding over your skin, on your lips, and sink into your body until you can't tell the difference between who you are and what you are witnessing–a complete surrender to the beauty of Earth herself. And every sunrise, sunset, moon rise is another chance to say thanks Mother Earth, you are so beautiful! So passed our trip from Honduras to Belize.

Belize has the 2nd largest reef system in the world; the first belonging to Australia. Passing through one of the very few breaks in that reef for the first time, in a 40' Vagabond Ketch can be extremely daunting. It was for me; one of those breathless moments when you forget the beauty all around you! I can't begin to tell you how much I appreciated Wayne's skill at maneuvering Merlin safely through. One of the first things we did, however, after safely passing through was to get stuck on one of the flats.

Imagine our joy when a couple of Belizean men came by and not only helped us maneuver out, but then guided us through to a safe anchorage. All we could do after anchoring was sit down and laugh at each other.

It was around Thanksgiving when we got to Belize and I was starving for a traditional Thanksgiving meal! The next day we went in to Customs & Immigration and began hunting for a turkey to cook on board. Wayne, Steve and I walked around the little town marveling at all the old buildings–run down or not they had a charm that was fascinating. We finally found a small turkey for sale in one of the largest grocery stores we'd seen for months and had quite a long discussion on whether or not we should buy it. There were only two there and finally, after much wheedling on my part, decided to go ahead and break the budget, which was exactly what the sale was fixing to do–it cost $50. I didn't care, I had made my mind up, we were going to have a traditional dinner for the first time in two years!

We loved Belize. The little nation was in a struggle at the time, trying to make the transition to a metropolitan, tourist attraction, and that was the only incongruent thing about it. Every tiny little cay within the reef system you could anchor at for days without seeing another person; the warm, sometimes even hot waters that made snorkeling a full day's activity; sometimes we'd watch a sleeping shark being cleaned off by a remora or other tiny fish that would usually be the shark's dinner; the fishermen who would bring conch shells over for us to look at; once again, we were in love with this planet we live on. No matter where you were in the Belizean waters, you couldn't help but run across a pool of dolphins. They were everywhere. One day I watched them cavorting way out across the bay coming towards us and I realized they were tossing something up in the air and playing ball with it! As they got closer, I recognized what it was–a plastic jug someone had evidently tossed away. It was so funny to watch them use it as a football! Belize was a Dolphin playground!

In one of the markets, I found Ricardo's Fish Seasoning, a mixture made there with, I suppose, lard & about 7 different seasonings including cayenne pepper and lime, that was so good it became a staple of ours, along with the coconut oil the ladies made in the villages. Inland were the jungles, the Mayan ruins that were part of the Mexican, Belizean, Guatemalan chain; there was also the leopard, jaguar, puma ocelot; the Howler monkeys and the people who seemed so quiet until the jump-ups and dancing began. Every time you fall in love with an island, a tiny nation, a new people you think it just can't get much better than this, but somehow, there you are, somewhere new and you fall in love all over again! And each time, I wonder, what if you found a way to keep this awe and joy alive in your life daily.

We moved Merlin across the flats, chewing nails the whole time, and anchored at Ambergris Caye; a tiny islet that had definite ideas of becoming a Coney Island/dive center for the entire area. Steve, although he didn't dive, and Wayne took off on a dive trip and I decided to walk the village get a feel for the place. It was way too commercial for me, even though it was too tiny to be so. There were shops selling dive gear, T-shirts, lava-lavas, more shops selling T-shirts and lava-lavas, sunglasses, hats & dive trips everywhere. But there was also ice cream! I walked around with a cone of chocolate ice cream, then butter scotch–great fun!

We spent three days there then ran across the flats again and anchored near town; we needed to make a trip to the airport and pick up Wayne's daughter, his brother and his gal. They had decided to finally get married, let Wayne perform the ceremony and spend their honeymoon with us. It was a pretty tight ship with the three of them, Steve, Wayne & I, not to mention our two cats. We spent a couple of weeks in and around the town, back and forth to Ambergris Cay, then finally headed down to the most southern point, Placencia for Christmas week. I cannot tell you how incredibly dreamy this little peninsula was with its palm lined beaches and coconut trees, surrounded by the turquoise waters of the Caribbean. When you hear about post-card picture perfect, you can't get much more like that in Plaencia. A most amazing thing happened as we pulled into anchor. Smorgasboard-morgie decided to choose that moment to go into labor. As we were trying to drop anchor, a dolphin came by and rubbed up against the hull; I often wondered if she heard or felt what was going on. It was a great beginning to the soon-to-be newlyweds and to one of our most favorite places. She gave birth to four cats that were soon to become great little sailors, and we opened a bottle of wine to celebrate.

It was such a magical time for everyone on board; we'd dingy out to the closest reefs, snorkel for the day, roam the village at night locating the best little cafes, meeting the villagers, sharing their stories; hiking back into the jungles.

All the little cafes (there were 3 of them) were local except one, which was owned by a German couple who had sailed in years before, dropped anchor, sold their boat and made Placencia their home. The trail that led to their little place started off at the beach, up a palm lined path in which all the palms leaned slightly forward as though they were trying to reach the ocean. Walking up the path in the moonlight or starlight was like walking thru a story book filled with gnomes and fairies, except the fairies were the phosphorescence drifting ashore as though they wanted to touch the palm trees. Just the walk to the little German café was enough to make you dreamy and wild eyed, warm and fuzzy. It was there, in Placencia that I learned of Boxing Day when, the day after Christmas, we saw all the villagers outside, walking together house to house with little tiny packages in their hands; packages of nuts, cookies, coconut oil, smoked fish, baked goods and all the trimmings. It was a happy, uplifting sight.

Way too soon, however, we had to make the trip back to Belize City, the main town and put everyone on the plane home. Even Steve had to go, he had contracted Malaria and was too sick to stay with us any longer. I was going to miss them terribly.

Wayne and I filled up with diesel, food and whatever else we needed then sailed to a tiny little anchorage we knew was small enough to handle only one boat at a time. It was a much-needed rest and we had finances to discuss. It was during this time that I experienced what could only be another incredible miracle.

After hours of speculating on whether we could, in fact, increase our finances, we came up with a plan that was remarkably simple, it fit our circumstances to a tee: we would offer our accommodations and hospitality for simple sailing vacations! It was perfect! And since we were certain of seeing plenty of dolphins on any trip we took, dolphins became a huge part of our advertising plan. We started planning out a brochure and Wayne came up with a picture of Merlin surrounded by dolphins with us and our cats looking overboard with great big huge smiles on our faces. I set my mind on the task of wording our perfectly inviting brochure....and we can guarantee you'll be surrounded by dolphins!

It's funny how things that were meant to be just happen with little or no effort; and things that we stumble onto soon grow to enormous weeds. Not even a week later I ran across a magazine entitled "Outside"; it was geared to every type of outside adventure you could ask for and its readers were huge. We decided to rake the money together to put a small ad in the back. It took quite a while for the brochure to come together and for us to get the money together. During that time, which was about 2 months, I began to notice something quite disturbing. Since beginning to put together the wording on the brochure, we had not come across one single dolphin. Not one. We decided to sail on south to Placencia, change our area; maybe we'd encounter them on the way down. But we didn't. Not a single one. I knew in my gut that something was wrong; day after day, sail after sail, there simply were no dolphins left in Belize, and that just simply couldn't be.

Finally, one day I walked back up to my favorite meditating spot, Merlin's bow, and sat down to ask:

"why, where are you, what happened?"

Within minutes came an answer with startling surprise..." you forgot to ask!"

Could it really be that simple, I thought; yet I knew without a doubt that that was exactly it. How huge must a heart be to consider the respect of all species, I thought. I formed a prayer-apology-thank-you-sorry-how-could I be so stupid- response and shook my head. Then I asked...

"if you hear me, please give me a sign, any sign at all, please." Within 5 minutes we were surrounded by dolphins.

I am fully aware of all the rebuttals to this exchange you might have, most of them come from me. Coincidence. Imagination. In fact, most of them start and end with either or, or sometimes both; it could really be nothing else. But all my life these coincidences had been happening, and all my life they have brought me closer and closer to that deep and rich sense of a greater existence. To my way of thinking, there had to be a reason for all this. But more than that, I knew in the very depth of my soul that this was not imagination or coincidence; it was real. I began to understand that the more one trusts, the more miracles one would experience; miracles were simply a manifestation of the willingness to be connected; again, I knew without a doubt that to doubt this, to decide it could not happen, was death...death to every greater sense we have. No matter how much Wayne screamed, he wasn't able to stop me from changing the wording on the brochure that the dolphins would be with us only if we asked them.

"Oh Christ, I can hear it now 'Hey Martha, I think we've got a crystal pusher animal huger here'... yeah, I can see they'll want to come sail with us!" He shouted.

Something else was beginning to creep into my thoughts; I started thinking of our sailing trips as a mini-chance to help others awaken to a greater sense. Without realizing it, I had just put Wayne's goals and mine at odds, I had just nailed one more rusty argument to our relationship.

"Look," I calmly explained, "maybe we can be more than just another rum drinking, get naked charter."

"We're broke! Save it for when you're rich then you can hire some bilge mopping young kid to help you save the world! Jeese!" he slammed his head with his fist.

We spent the next month sailing back and forth from Belize to Guatemala, learning the area and becoming familiar with the waters. I wish I could give you a picture of the Rio Dulce River in Guatemala; anchored within the walls of green jungle forest, it felt as though we were anchored within the arms of the Great Mother herself. There is a sound within the silence of a massive jungle sleeping at night with the breath of creatures all around you and the pull and tug of a river current that, in its own liquid way, grounds you as surely as the earth herself; waking to Howler Monkeys and jungle creatures in the early morning sunrise–it is humbling and provocative, thrilling and quieting all at the same time. Some of you may know that the Rio Dulce River area in Guatemala is where the first Tarzan movies were filmed; it's understandable! I had fallen in love, yet again, everywhere I looked, the face of the Goddess, Mother Earth surrounded me.

Within months we received our first charter, then our second and third. It seemed we were well on our way to doing something that was economically good for us and fulfilling! We had so many amazing charters, so many incredible people on our boat; couples, families, groups who had vowed to meet once a year somewhere different; those who only wanted to fish, those with questions we had no answers to; some who expected catering and pampering we were unable to give, others so amazed by every nuance, every chance to take the wheel, every islander, every Mayan washing laundry along the river bed villages, every creature we came upon, every night at anchor and day at sail that they cried when they left. With the help of Mother Earth, we touched a place in the hearts of people that had not been touched before. I would never forget this.

In the southernmost tip of the Rio Dulce is a community of ex-pats; they own hotels, restaurants, bars or have simply come to lay down their anchors and hang out for the remainder of their lives, and some people simply filled with secrets. Within that circle of friends and acquaintances was a readymade home if we wanted it. It was not without its problems; divorce, subterfuge, drunkenness, competition for your business, and the ever-ever present problem of "acceptable pay to the locals". I broke that one when I paid an eager, young Mayan girl $5 to clean the inside of Merlin.

"Totally unacceptable, do you realize what you have just done?" voiced one irate man with a half full beer in his hands.

"It takes just one jerk to undermine the entire economy we stand on, don't 'ya know?" said another.

The going rate was $2.00 a boat, or a house, or a day. Honestly, it was not my intention to disrupt this Pharoistic harmony; I actually thought $5.00 was pretty cheap!

Wayne and I took our charters back and forth between Belize and Guatemala for about six months, traveled inland into Chichicastenega, up into the mountains where the boiling sulfur pools were piped into your rooms; the roads so steep and winding, the buses so full that whenever they tipped a little too far to the left and right, we all just leaned the other way and kept it upright! We came upon villages that still honored their ancient ways in their dress, their customs, and rituals; we saw Shamans sitting at the back of a Christian church taking offerings from their people; caskets paraded through town and turned around and around so the dead would not be able to find their way back, then brought to the church for burial. It seemed as though the Christians and Mayans had found a strong sense of balance between their ideas and life styles. And it seemed as though we were settled into a perfectly balanced live style–doing something we loved, making enough money to keep it going and to enjoy our lives; learning every day from the earth, the sea and the people who surrounded us.

We decided to spend a season in Guatemala, it was summer in the states and charters were less and less. I spent some time in the Tikal area of Guatemala, among the

Mayan ruins and gravitated towards the Temple of the Priestess. It was while I was standing at the top, surrounded by clouds and the upper atmosphere of the sky that I began to see a scene unfolding–the Priestess stepping slowly down the steep steps of the pyramid, descending from the sky to the earth, ready to perform the fertile rituals of spring, the people gathered around for the celebration. Instinctively I understood the connection they had with their Gods and Goddesses, the connection they understood they were a part of. It was not a feeling of isolated or personal power, but one of responsibility and love. It was an unexpected feeling.

Around a year later, while in the little village/town on the Rio Dulce River, Guatemala, I noticed a huge throng of Mayans gathered around a little shop. These Mayans, for the most part, lived in the mountains surrounding the River and came to town once a month to sell, buy or trade for what they needed; it took them approximately 2 days to walk down from their mountain homes. They were all watching a television that sat in the window; they were mesmerized, standing there, eyes peeled to the set; I can't remember what was playing. Later that evening I learned from a man in the local bar that his company had put the television in the window and let it play for the whole village. It turned out his company was a British Oil firm that was working with the government to secure rights to drill for oil in the Rio Dulce River–the television was one of the offerings from the company to placate the villagers, along with a school and if they absolutely had to, they'd build a hospital. This river was a life blood to those who lived there, they fished from it, swam in it, gathered roots or food and thatch. We argued for almost an hour about the ethics of this offer, the damage to the river, their fish and other needs, compared to one free television and one school in a village they would only go to once or twice a month.

He ended the conversation with one quip, "Apparently you don't want these people to have the same luxuries you have, do you?"

I was stunned; what do you say to that? It was a jaunty-company-man-made-media-spin I just wasn't ready for and I've always wished I had a rocking good come back to shout at him–something intelligent like "You friggin idiot!"

So back and forth we'd go from the waterfalls, rivers and village life to the ex-pat community; back and forth from the lush wild jungles to rumors of whose wife was sleeping with what's-his-name; no one ever mentioned what's-his-name sleeping with someone's wife! Weird! Back and forth between Howler Monkeys, parrots and women selling freshly prepared tortillas to the reality of Susana's French Bar and Grill at war with some other bar and grille; it was like a slap in the face each time, a whiplash of realities. Wayne didn't seem to mind it, it was just everyday normal reality to him (and to everyone else, I guess), but there it was again, that sense that this reality we believed simply was–always will be, carved in stone, began to disintegrate, shimmer like a mirage, the more I embraced my women's sense. The more I saw life thru the eyes of a woman, through the soul of the Goddess, it just simply began to fall apart. The very earth we took for granted was in fact, the living manifestation of the harmony, grace and relationship bliss we all claim to be looking for; she was in fact our teacher!

It was at Susana's we had one of our last arguments.

"Something's going on, Wayne. Something that's blocking our spiritual connection to Earth. I don't like it. It isn't truth" I began, carefully. Maybe we could get through this one.

"There is no spiritual connection. You just have to understand that, the two don't mix. That's why we're given the promise of delivery."

I should have understood immediately what the enormous difference between us was and why we were having such a hard time communicating. Wayne fundamentally believed spirituality was linked, in its entirety, to the bible; there simply was nothing spiritual about Earth, and especially a Goddess. We were two, blind, opposing forces. I should have stopped right then. I should have got it right then, but I didn't. So I kept going.

"Delivery? From What? Double rainbows, sunsets no painting can ever match. Herbs that heal, trees bearing fruit, toys, rope, cloth, instruments? Mountain streams, snowcapped peaks, canyons? Or are you talking about the hunger, war, homeless; you know, all the things we ourselves bring about. Hey, by the way, are we taking all that war and hunger with us to heaven, or are we just going to leave it down here to rot?"

"You are so damn antagonistic!" He got up and walked away.

Looking back on it now, a little wiser, a bit more tolerant, I understand my part in bringing about the horrible end to Wayne's & my relationship; my head hanging down over the cockpit combing, his hands around my throat, squeezing with rage; it was an ending no larger than the larger than life style we were living. I had become preachy, floundering, trying to find my balance in a world filled with wonder and possibilities. I demanded that he saw what I saw, felt what I felt and he couldn't. Perhaps wouldn't, not yet, not then. And so it ended, with neither of us fully capable of looking each other in the eye.

I'd like to share with you, however, a final episode in Wayne's & my life. It happened in Hawaii, sometime after he and I had split, but to do so, I need to step back to a year before we left to go sailing. We had spent a couple of weeks in New Orleans enjoying the rich, wild and sensuous nature of that incredible city. I loved Cameo rings and he ought me one, surrounded by a tiny strand of pearls. During our time at sea, the ring had broken so many times I finally put it in a plastic bag and stowed it away. When I left Merlin, I couldn't find it anywhere; it was as though it had vanished as thoroughly as our love for each other...or so I thought. I had been in Hawaii for approximately three years and there had been a lengthy interlude since I had last talked with Wayne–almost 2 years.

One night I had a dream...

Merlin and Ko'Lea were resting side by side in a calm, vast ocean; bows slightly pointed towards each other. It was neither sunny nor gray, more like an enchanted mixture of both. Merlin was in all black, silk black, the rigging, the sails, the mast and hull. Ko stood beside him in opalescent, shimmering white. Had they been human, they would have been holding hands, eyes closed, deep in meditation. A sad quiet blessedness both surrounded and emanated from them. They were at peace...

I had a strange feeling about it, but for the life of me, I couldn't figure out what it meant. While talking to Steve on the phone the next day he informed me that Wayne had a heart attack and passed away the year before. I was so shocked and saddened. I couldn't believe it had happened, couldn't believe I had spent the last year or so not knowing. But I finally understood my dream.

I got into my dingy and slowly rowed back to my boat, hopped on board, went to my stateroom and began to sob. Everything that had gone wrong with us went tumbling thru my mind and with it a heavy grief for us, our time together. I just poured out

'Wayne, I'm so sorry we couldn't make it, it wasn't your fault; I'm just so sorry for everything that went wrong.'

After crying for what seemed like the entire morning, I felt lighter, but still weepy. I turned to make my bunk and as I was straightening the sheets, there in the middle of the bed, was the pearl encased cameo ring he had bought me; it was intact, healed, fixed and out of its plastic holder. The tears began again, this time for sheer joy; I thanked him for the message.

# Chapter 10—Life After Guatemala

What can I say about Penny–Penelope W. Some people can only be experienced; even the most extraordinary words become trite when used to explain the enormous power and humility, intelligence and child-like innocence, with total grace that flowed like a raging river from women like Penny. When I left Guatemala she took me in with no questions asked and my eyes opened to the world of a true healer. Her abilities to heal came not just from her hands, but her very essence. Being around her could change one's perspective from depression or upset to joy and hope, quick as whiplash.

But with all her own healing abilities, her greatest dream was to bring the experience of healing to others in any way she could. I was blessed to experience a Faith healer she brought in from the Philippines (also called Psychic Surgeons). It was a phenomenal experience. She opened her house and heart to any who wanted/needed healing. Till her dying breath, she dreamed of opening a Center that would bring together all types of healers—allopathic, homeopathic, naturopathic; crystal and energy healing; counseling, mediums; she had no judgment of who or what was better, what was real or woo-woo. She believed only in the power to heal whatever the body, mind and soul needed. She believed in the power of love.

Why introduce you to her? Bring her into my story? Because I'm not sure my story would ever be complete without her being in my life. She gave me the experience of unconditional love; she set the bar so high on living without judgment. She was my living, breathing real life example of the Divine Feminine, and our Mother Earth.

Her Center never came to be. Penny had cancer. She made the decision to follow her heart and take the path of natural healing and for 21 years she rode the wave of health and relapse, of rebound and collapse; astounding a plethora of doctors and healers who could only shake their heads at the miracle she was. I suppose I also needed to learn that each of us, no matter how high our bar was or is, has demons. Penny could never face hers–the emotional pain she carried from childhood, though she tried so hard to banish it. She could never set boundaries so the act of giving, giving, always giving without return took a devastating toll on her heart and body. Yes, I was one of those tolls; I could not give her what she needed at the time. Perhaps one of the greatest life lessons we learn, if we are lucky, is forgiveness. Especially self-forgiveness.

I wonder now, if that is part of what is happening to our Mother Earth right with all the climate change, fires, super storms. Although we are blindly unaware of it, She gives everything we need to live–food, clothing, medicines; even music, definitely poetry, inspiration and beauty. But throughout most of our time here on Earth, we have taken it all and given little in return. Do you think all our global problems are an indication that her body and soul are now suffering greatly because of it?

# Chapter 11–Moving on

Eventually I sold the building my cafe resided in, back in Flagstaff, for a lump sum. Enough to move to Hawaii and put a down payment on my own boat. How I loved Hawaii! I felt the presence of Spirit, the Divine Feminine and Divine Male everywhere I looked and everywhere I touched. I hadn't felt that much power since Hopi land. But the sensual, raw beauty of those islands spoke the clearest and loudest message–here was the life of Mana, the power of an ancient tongue spoken through feelings, beauty, insights and instincts; here was a Spiritual Power born of the land, reaching out to connect to all. Communal, tribal. Here was the Goddess. Again, I felt the desperate need to regain that ancient tongue, Mother Tongue. I wanted to sit down and write a poem about a tribe of women who could speak that Mother tongue, who could hear Her voice and transcribe it into some exquisite, liquid jewel that just pours from their lips, then pours into our minds, our hands and into all we are related with; leaving us with this amazing wisdom, this ancient knowledge that spins our world upside down–it is time to bring this knowledge, this wisdom, this essence back into our world.

Hawaii, I discovered, is all about balance. Balance between male and female, between spirit and man/woman kind; balance in everything worldly and spiritual. I have long since felt that we are and have been so out of balance that it appears to us to be 'normal'. For so long I've felt that to bring back the balance, we'd have to start with what we had always before thought of as Spiritual.

We need to hear the voice of the wise woman Priestess again. Not the voice of a woman who has been given the 'equal right' to teach the word of God, but the voice of one who will speak the words of the Goddess. I love to think on those words. Real words, not words about life after death, or living in fear for your mortal soul, but words about a functional planet, living with integrity, in harmony, balance, and joy right here on earth. Words about an education that teaches about the prosperity of giving back, the wealth of caring for each other, the riches of peace! Colleges that give degrees in sustainable, symbiotic abundance for all; I think on these words and realize that I'm speaking like a woman! These are, however, words of a woman who remembers her legacy as an Ambassador of The Mother, her link between nature and mankind, a keeper of the vision of balance and harmony. I am proud to think like a woman!

On Oahu I spotted my boat, Ko 'Lea. She was the most beautiful sight I'd ever seen; a 34' Panda, stay sail cutter with teak inside and out and I couldn't wait to make her my own. I called her Ko for short. I didn't know then that we'd spend the next 9 years together sailing around Hawaii, then to Tarawa, then to Micronesia. She was my sister and my best friend! I was lucky enough to find an anchorage in one of the bays outside Lanai where the Iao Valley Mountains watched over us during the day, and every sunrise and sunset greeted us with blazing streaks of fire. At night we rocked softly with the waves, enveloped in the silence under the ever-loving gaze of stars and moon. It was an incredible time, well, except for the winter storms that raged through the anchorage like a mad man threatening to tear every mast, every boat, every dingy to the bottom of the ocean. While trying to row back to his boat in one of these storms, a friend in the anchorage was blown across the bay to the island of Lanai. While the story was remarkable, I was very glad it was his story, and not mine!

During my 5 ½ years in Hawaii, I finally began to understand something that had been slipping in and out of my conscience for ages. It may seem unreal to you, but I ask that you suspend disbelief long enough to hear me out. There is a voice which emanates from the land and its beauty that, as one begins to surrender to it, can be heard as clear as the voice of your best friend. Maybe it comes as inspiration, or guidance from a greater source, I'm not sure. I've come to know it as the Spiritual Manna of Beauty–Pua Mana, in the words of the Hawaiians. Suddenly the ancient powers of the Kahuna, the Hopi Priests and Healers, the Wise Women of old we call Witches became very clear; it wasn't just from the teachings that were handed down through the ages that gave them their personal power, but from their close proximity to Earth, their ability to listen and hear what was all around them, their willingness to dance and sing in prayer. It was and still is the Mother Tongue. Sadly, it also explained why so much of magic of life has been lost.

I have so many heartwarming memories from Hawaii, like:

- a predawn row into harbor, just before the sunrise, watching those breathless moments when the depth of colors start to shift and alter into silvers, indigo, rose;

- while sitting in the cockpit, swaying in the ocean waves, watching a rainbow begin to grow and rise up between two peaks in the Iao Valley Mountains;
- anchored in a tiny cove, watching a waxing moon rise and literally hearing the cacophony of stars herald her welcome', being overcome by the enormity of it;
- swimming out to reach a pod of wild dolphins and watch them react to me, curious, playful, willing, wondering;
- walking down a secret trail hidden with ferns and flowering ginger to a swimming hole only a few knew of, or the waterfalls and jungle of Hanna where the past, present and hopefully the continued future all merge into wonderland;
- sitting at sunset under the gigantic, ancient Banyan Tree in Lahaina listening to the chatter of birds talking of their day, and knowing without a doubt that I am in their world, not the other way around;
- sailing with Haiku friends, loaded down with songs, mini congas, green papaya salad and Hawaiian chants, right into the heart and heat of the humpback whales;
- screaming with ecstasy as they raced and stormed thru the waters, rising up alongside Ko, scaring the piss out everyone on board;
- the amazement of watching a mother whale bring her baby to Ko's side and play for an hour, the baby peeking out from mom's flanks, swimming underneath, coming up on the other side–so

trusting, so curious, wanting to be with us as much as we wanted to be with her;

· being awakened in the middle of the night, running out from my bunk to get topside because a mother whale was singing to her babe, and the babe answering back.

· walking down the street and hearing that voice say 'put flowers in your hair, put the ocean in your walk';

· a full moon night-hike into the crater of Haleakala;

· hearing the sound of the conch, watching the grace of the hula dancers on a beach and joining in with drums and rattles.


Hawaii, like so many of the islands I'd visited, was not just a nice place to vacation; if you surrendered to it, you came away with 'a life', beating in your heart and soul. I had a long standing confrontation with so many who claimed that in order to be intelligent and grounded you needed shut down your senses, your intuition; use your head instead of feelings; they can deceive you, confuse you, demean you; you could become unbalanced! The years I spent in Hawaii, ripped that lie away and drowned it in her healing waters; replacing it with clear, wide open eyes and a Woman's intuitive knowledge of intelligence:

· you cannot be fully grounded or intelligent without opening all your senses, to close them off leaves you unbalanced, living only a half-life;

- if you live only a half-life, you will only be able to see our Mother Earth as something to dominate, to own, to possess;
- if you walk thru beauty, unable to see the what truly is, then the only thing you will see are condos, concrete, and resorts–which are then made into a 'look-alike-picture-post-card'    of the living, breathing earth you just plowed under;
- or worse–just possibly the worse that I can now imagine–you will only see our incredible planet as something to be delivered from! Arrgh!

It was in Maui that I stumbled onto The Maui Live Poet Society, and was awakened to my own ability to write poetry. Never in my life did I believe I could actually write and perform poetry, but wow, it stormed into my life like a hot, steaming lover. Another one of Hawaii's gifts. So now I am burdened with books and books of hand-written poetry, some great, some dreadful, but I can't seem to them toss out. Many early ones influenced by my lover in the society who also stormed into my life like a hurricane. We were inseparable, inspirational, scandalous lovers, totally headed for disaster! Embracing each other with lips, arms and words; devil-may-care lovers who wrote thinly veiled lines of love making, promises and outrageous wet kisses on every street in Lahaina. Until jealousy, possession and rage took over on the new moon, in the middle of the beautiful Maui waters. He tried to cut the hoses that would cause Ko to sink. I tried to hit him over the head with a frying pan. He failed and I failed, and our passion sunk into horror as we realized what we'd become. I never regretted knowing and loving Lawrence; he was an enormously gifted poet. He once roused a crowd of 100+ people into a standing ovation with his poetry. I could have loved him forever, but I had finally learned that lesson we all learn eventually-I could not and will not tolerate physical and mental abuse, even if it came from God himself.

After Lawrence and my relationship dissolved into a muddy puddle, I felt it was time to move on, time for me to begin sailing again. I met Roberta a few years back and we became strong, fast friends. She took people out into the ocean to swim with wild dolphins and to enjoy the whales. We had a lot in common. Roberta was a tall, slender beauty with brown hair and elvish ears. When she smiled, she actually looked like a dolphin! She had worked with John Lilly (the man who discovered that dolphins were involuntary breathers) for years before going out on her own and had a powerful relationship with the Cetacean Nation. But she was having a major discourse with her husband and her life at that time, so she decided to join me and go sailing around the world for a while. With her four-year-old son!

We outfitted Ko with net all around the railings hoping to keep a wild four-year-old on the decks while under sail. We packed the Ko with enough supplies to last a month, bought charts, books, a hand held GPS, and whatever else we could think of to make the trip safe and still fun! We put in Jiffy Reefing and an automatic pilot, then after a month of planning and practice sails, set on our way.

Our first stop ended up being Tarawa, about 2 degrees south of the equator. Upon arrival, I radioed in to Immigration's and they asked to speak to the Captain.

"That would be me!". I said, delighted to speak up.

"No man aboard?" he asked.

"No sir, just us two woman and one child" I was getting a bit of a weird feeling about the conversation. Two days passed and still they had not come aboard to check our papers. I called again asking for direction. Should we come to shore? Should we just move on? This was not what I expected for my first call at a foreign port.

Finally, the next day they radioed that they would be there by 11:00 a.m. And they were; Immigration Officer, Customs, Port Captain, and about 2 other officials and some others I had no idea of who they were. They checked our papers, passports, then checked Ko out thoroughly. We waited patiently until they finally sat down and started stamping away. Finally, the Port Captain, who was fairly good looking by the way–stark blue eyes, a mass of softly graying hair, well built, and a great accent–looked at me and spoke up.

"We are very sorry ma'am for the delay. But you must understand that this is very remarkable. 2 women sailing alone?" he began. Then he laughed, shook his head, and continued. "We thought you may have killed your husbands and took the boat by force, just weren't sure what we would do!"

I honestly didn't know how to answer that. "Ah, well, I have no husband and Roberta's husband is in Hawaii, safe and sound"

Now I know you may not believe this, but it's all true. Even what happened next. One of the men spotted my guitar leaning against the couch and asked if he could play it. Another asked if we had anything to drink. Around 4:00 I decided I'd better make supper for us all because they didn't seem any too eager to leave. Spaghetti. And Gin and tonics, and some of the best guitar playing I've heard come from my old cheap guitar. It was a great day! And we were finally welcomed to their island. Never in all the time Wayne and I sailed did we encounter such a crazy check in at a port of call!

# Chapter 12-The Four Matriarchs

On our 2nd day ashore, we met a local man named Denly. Denly was a politician, both literally and emotionally. He took us under his wing and introduced us to so many people it was hard to keep up. But we loved every minute of his beguiling nature, easy manners, and fat, robust body; he had a wild mop of brown/gray hair that looked pretty good pulled back into a tight fisted ponytail, but looked outrageously inconsiderate left hanging out, as did his belly; sort of like something one should be embarrassed to look at, but nevertheless, looks at anyway!. He clapped shoulders and shook hands across the entire island and he never stopped talking. So, each time he re-told the story of these two single women sailing across the ocean alone, except for a four-year-old, we only had to smile and nod as he spewed forth on to another story. Over dinner one night he proposed a journey to his home island of Marakei. It was a crazy thing for us to agree to. We'd only known him for a couple of days. It was ludicrous, stupid, and dangerous. But most of all it was miraculous!

You couldn't take a boat to Marakei, it had no harbor and no way to anchor. So we had to take a little puddle jumper plane to get there. I remember piling on board with 10 other passengers watching the pilot use the strength of her arms and body to get the door closed. Roberta and I looked at each other with raised eyebrows and a little bit of sweat.

I wish I could paint you a picture of Marakei, there just aren't any words to describe the jewel this tiny atoll is.

There is one narrow road that circles an inland sea of azure blues and greens with palm trees and coconut trees and flowers of all kinds and colors. When we disembarked the plane, we had to wait quite a long time. There was only one truck on the whole island and 2 scooters. Most of the passengers had bikes left at the tiny hut that served as an airport, or they simply walked to their destination. Denly left to get the scooters then he and another man took us to the Chief's dwelling where we would be lodging with the Chief's family. At that time, there were no other lodgings except with the villagers themselves. But first of all, we needed to be presented to the villagers, then finally presented to the Four Matriarchs. They were the ones who would give the final approval on whether or not we could stay. It was a scary thought, who were these people? Lunch, however was served and we were starving! So there Roberta, Joey and I sat, alone at a huge round table, while the clan stood all around us watching us eat. Aren't there horror movies that have this plot? Roberta and I were both thinking the same thing. When we finally began to eat were very pleased–fish, rice, plantains, coconut sauce and coconut water. OK, we got through this one!

We each jumped on the back of a scooter, Denly and I in front, Roberta and Joey on the other one. We were on our way to be presented to the villagers. Village after village we stopped, got off and sat in front of women and children who just assessed us, nodding their heads and giggling to each other. They used their own language so we didn't know what was being said, but Denly explained that they were wondering if we had come to search for husbands. Perhaps that's why there weren't any men around. Each village greeted us with a fresh coconut to drink, pandamas mats to sit on, and honestly, we were overwhelmed with the warmth and graciousness of these island people.

So we'd scoot along, stop, get gawked at and critiqued, then scoot along again. The smell of late afternoon wood smoke, tropical blossoms and that singular tropical bush smell that permeates the air, the soil and breath of all islands everywhere mingled together with the sound of bird, breeze and child chatter. Within the heart of all this lay a sleepy emerald lagoon; a secret place where men and children became one, fishing, playing, moving in and out of sunlight and shadow, all surrounded by palms, hibiscus and taro leaves reaching up like some giant plant life beast of prey, in protection of their tiny hidden gem.

Finally, after 4 villages, it was time to meet the Matriarchs. For whatever reason, I had put tobacco and some crystals in my pocket before leaving, not knowing what an appropriate gift would be to present to the Matriarchs, just knowing I had to have something to give to these elders.

Denly and the other gentleman, named James finally pulled into what seemed a deserted path that I could only imagine led inward towards the lagoon. We started walking and Denly was very quiet. Actually, neither I nor Roberta could imagine talking at this point, the path simply had a 'be quiet' feel to it. We rounded a corner and there she stood. A beautifully carved stone statue of a Crone with her hands held high watching over the lagoon. Yes, I was stunned, yet something in me instinctively knew it was never going to be a real person. There were four of them standing watch in sacred spots around the lagoon. A Mother, a Maiden, the Crone and the fourth was a child. I was looking at the islander's past, at something sacred; their ancient belief in the Goddess, the Mother who kept watch over this precious and gorgeous lagoon. Denly explained that even tho most of the island was Christian now, they still felt a great reverence for the Four Matriarchs. They had stood there forever to keep the lagoon safe from any outsider who would harm it. I could feel the sacred energy all around me. I needed to bow my head and show respect; I felt so at home here, surrounded by a lagoon sparkling like a jewel holding within its arms a benevolent presence that felt huge and powerful. I placed some of the tobacco in a niche within the Crone's statue, and some at the Mother's. The crystals I knew were for the young girl and child. We had to get back on the scooters to reach them though, they were way on the other side of the lagoon. Two narrow channels link the lagoon with the ocean, allowing fish to enter. Denly related some ancient legends that surrounded the statues—one of the fisherman who sneaked into the lagoon from the ocean, and the Crone turned herself into a sea monster and dragged him to the bottom of the lagoon. Another time the Maiden became flesh and lured the interloper back out to sea then brought on a storm to keep him away. But this wasn't the only mystery we would witness on this precious island.

The next day we were to attend a huge island celebration for the opening of their new hospital. There was food strewn across 4 tables, all from the villages we had visited and those we never got to–fish fried, broiled, cervichi; gummy balls made from coconut gel, bananas mashed into rice, and plenty else. Some of which I tasted, then had to carefully spit into my napkin! Coconut water for the youngsters and some strange tasting beverage the islanders made from sap. It was intoxicating! We listened to speeches, watched dancers parade from each village. We ate and drank (sparingly). Then later in the evening we were blessed with the presence of one of the most isolated villages on the island. This village believed that, long long ago, a huge sea eagle had come down and mated with one of the village girls. From that union most of their clan were born. The sea eagle gave them a dance to perform that they alone could do. It was believed that if they did it correctly, they would go into a trance and see the sea eagle for themselves. They were going to perform the dance for us all. It was a strange dance, feet stomping, hands raised, heads swirling to the music, always in motion, moving around each other faster and faster. Then one young girl began to tremble, and fell down into a stupor. She began calling out in their strange language and I knew she had seen her eagle.

I knew there were so many religions around the world that had their dances of ecstasy and it would be so easy to pass this off as just another display of religious fervor, but I was mesmerized by her glow of peace and joy as they removed her from the floor. I couldn't cheapen what she felt with doubts and snickers. Sometime later I was asked to say a few words about us and what brought us here. All I can remember was stumbling through some words about feeling we were led here, meant to be here, and how grateful I was to be blessed by our time here on this little island. Marakei, a precious living jewel, a tiny atoll in the middle of the ocean which still held fast to their ancient traditions and their immeasurable beauty.

I have since learned that they started building causeways that have resulted in lowering oxygen in the lagoon. The water has become stagnant and there are no more fish in the lagoon. Each time I think of Marakei, I offer a prayer of gratitude that I was lucky enough to experience Her before that happened. Wikipedia describes the 4 Matriarchs as the four ghosts of Marakei; I wonder what Denly would think of that! I wonder if The Goddess rolls her eyes every time someone reads that!

# Chapter 13—Saying Good-bye Again

When we returned to Tarawa, Roberta decided she needed to go back to Hawaii. Joey's grandfather was dying and I think she had grown tired of sailing. I felt so alone as she boarded the plane, as we hugged and said our good-byes.

I hung around Tarawa for about a month before setting my leave date. I was stalling and I knew it! I wasn't even sure where I wanted to go...Samoa? Polynesia? Vanuatu? I couldn't drudge up enough energy to get excited about any of them. I started reading about some tiny islands closer to me called Micronesia and fell in love with one called Kosrae. After meeting with a New Zealander family sailing with their 2 kids, aboard their boat called "Fellowship", I was further intrigued when they announced they were going to Kosrae next.

We started hanging out together, going for walks, then over to Fellowship for tea–I thought tea was a drink, turns out it's an early dinner! One hot afternoon, we all decided to go get ice cream at the local kids' place. Millie decided she had some personal shopping to do so with a conspiratorial grin, she took my hand and we walked in the other direction.

"Meet you at the ice cream shop!" she called over her shoulder. "There's plenty of time, let's just keep peeking in all these little stores. You find the most amazing things, as long as you don't need anything particular, that is."

Within a half hour we were knee high in some pretty ridiculous for-future-birthday-party trinkets that were so out of touch, they looked like a latest fad.

"Look at this. When was the last time you wore bloody purple pop beads?" She said.

"Or," I lifted them up to show her "ruffled ink panties! I had some when I was a kid even showed them off in church."

"Cuff Links?"

"Earrings, I think." I shook my head looking at them.

"They'll do very nicely." Millie's bag was beginning to pooch a bit, but she kept on stuffing goodies into it. "Can always do with another deck of girlie cards."

"And some bright red, plastic butterfly clips for the hair" I dropped them in her purse.

"A couple of adjustable diamond rings. Now here's a find–a pack of candy cigarettes. What do you think?"

"No Surgeon General's warning...has been known to cause tooth decay, sibling disputes, and future unacceptable social habits." I bit my tongue, I still smoked. "I don't know, you gotta leave some discoveries for later life."

Finally loaded down, we set off to meet with the rest of the group and gobble up some ice cream.

"What's this?" Millie cried.

"The one and only war memorial on the island. It's a plaque for all the Australians and Americans who fought on the islands during the war." I answered softly.

"I've never liked these memorials!" she said quite adamantly. "It's like teaching your children war is some kind of accomplishment."

"What? You don't want to send Jimmy to some academy to, what do they say, gain the discipline life needs?

"What an easy way out. May the powers that be give Steve and I the strength to accomplish that ourselves. It's an issue we have to face soon." We walked away from the memorials before Millie continued.

"It's just so hard to balance what's going on today with what you feel; you constantly worry about peer pressure your children will face. You preach peace, their friends want to play video war games. I bloody swear, there's some brand-new line of commando-born-to-kill just begging to be taken home-as a Christmas gift mind you!" You could tell she was angry, head down, face slightly red.

"Conscious Consumerism, I think that's how we have to beat it." I added.

"Lovely words" she snapped "lovely. I think of it more as a mother's gut instinct. It doesn't take a bloody analyst to figure out it's combat you're putting in your child's mind." You could tell she didn't think much of the "bloody analyst".

We walked a while more, we had about three blocks to go. The sun looked so hot I thought it would blow up. Our conversation drifted in and out of newscasts, what we learn in school vs. what we learn in life. Eventually we even wandered into women vs. men's thinking. I felt comfortable enough to mention my thoughts on looking at life through the eyes of a woman rather than our usual patriarchal ways of thinking.

"Oh bloody hell, yes!" she laughed. "Although I've never heard it put like that, I know exactly what you mean! And don't you think there are so many women afraid to go there?"

"Well, yeah; for so long we've been taught that to be accepted you have to think like a man, and you know what happens then..." we both said at the same time "keep doing the same thing over and over and you'll just get the same results over and over!" We were both laughing at that.

"Although I do sometimes think that without men, we perhaps would never have progressed as we have. I suppose Patriarchy does have its points." She mused.

"I don't believe that, Millie," I said. "The technological progression that comes from our minds is a natural thing. It would have happened either way. We would have progressed, but we would have done it in a totally different way."

"Hmmm," she answered. "Let me think about that"

Steve, Millie and I roamed about Tarawa for a couple of days filling up with diesel, propane, junk food to snack on for the trip. I finally got my auto-pilot fixed, thanks to a young German man who lived in Tarawa, packed loads of food and a sack of oranges and tangerines (sometimes it's all you want to eat on board) and set my date to leave on Saturday.

I wanted to clean up Ko before leaving, and clear out all the mud wasps that had made homes inside the cabin. It had taken me a while to realize they were harmless and the little homes they built were absolutely fascinating. Little two-story mud condos, with a dead spider inside so when the babies hatched, they'd have something to eat. Please don't ask me why I was so fascinated with them...I just found myself mesmerized every time I took one apart. Finally, after clearing the mud wasps out I hauled up the anchor and headed out to sea; stalling had to come to an end.

Maybe it's a sailor's thing, but did you ever notice how, when anyone starts to head out to the big blue, a sudden largess of well-wishers come around to say '...man, did you see that movie about the boat that sunk...' Alas, every imaginable catastrophe began happening inside my head; husky Caribbean pirates were suddenly transformed into North Pacific Asian drug lords, frayed sails and broken masts replaced the sugar plums and candy canes in dreams. I wish I could tell you that I was raring to go, a brave young woman, sporting a brave young woman's courage and certainty, but I wasn't. Inside I was sporting a massive dose of uncertainty! Fear, doubt, and an oppressive sense of self-worth. But I kept going, hauled up Ko's main sail, and steered my way out of the anchorage that had been my home for the past 3 months. Although I had sailed alone in Hawaii, captained a crew across the Hawaii chain, and got us to Tarawa safely, I had never actually been out on the open ocean waters by myself, alone, just me and Ko. Butterflies were making themselves a nest inside my tummy, as I hauled up Ko's stay sail until I finally settled down to my first evening's meal of oranges and chocolate; all under a communal sky of liquid sapphire and a setting sun of emeralds and garnets. Finally, I entered the first words of my sailor's log turned personal journal: *Forgot how much I hate soggy downwind sailing, Ko looks like she's drunk.* Think I got my whimsy back, actually felt the presence of Mother Ocean watching, waiting, (does seem like there's some kind of bond between Mother Earth/Ocean with her daughters) while I set the sails and the compass course for some tiny speck of land, some huge speck of perspective. Kosrae, Island of the Sleeping Lady; now there's something to ponder. 600 NM. to the northwest.

I decided to stay up nights, watching for any sister boats that may be out there. I'd sleep during the day, or at least most of it. It's funny what you hear at night, a cacophony of sounds that you know can't really be there, but they are. Some are the sound of wind in the rigging, some just the creaking of the boat, but others are like voices; you can't tell what they are whispering, but you can hear them. Soft undertones like those you may hear in the next apartment, or a closed off closet. I listened to them that first night, and the second night wondering if I was hearing the voices of all the sailors who have passed this way before me. I didn't feel quite so alone as I listened to those sounds. The 3rd night out I was smack in the middle of some meteor shower. Thousands of thousands of stars lighting up the sky like fireworks on the 4th of July! I didn't know what I was watching, but I felt as tho I had just sailed into some mystical universe that had exploded just for Ko and I. It was breathtaking! Outrageous. Gorgeous. I felt like the luckiest girl alive!

Maybe it's the balance one feels out here, but you get the feeling that everything around you is alive with

111

personality. The water, the way it moves; a sensual independent female rising and tossing with the moons' transit. And the sun, a hot morning lover, come to stoke up the fire, turn on the heat for some late afternoon sweat and melt down, until you need to cool down, until he moves lowdown in the sky, giving up the night time. I mean you gotta love him as he tips his top hat, tosses his rose-colored tails and slips across the sky, as all proper lords should, and quite often do. Leaving behind a promise of fine sparkling diamonds that may fall from the sky, may fall from his wake. Leaving all us ladies, Ko, the moon, the ocean and me alone to rule the night. Our night. Left alone to sing, howl, sail, dream and fly through the visions of our very own dimensions. So I just sat back, and watched the diamonds explode through the night sky and occasionally opened up my palm to see if one fell.

The next night I noticed a light in the water following me. It would light up, drift around Ko, then suddenly go dark, then light up again and drift around Ko for what seemed 5 minutes or so. I watched this phenomenon for quite a while. It was in the shape of a Ray, yet I knew of no Rays this far out in the ocean. It kept me company all night long. Some sea creature I was sure of that. It reminded me of a series of 3 dreams I had about rays:

> I was giving a tarot reading to a remarkable redhead when all of a sudden, we heard a great commotion coming out from a canal near us. There they came out of the water, standing straight up like ancient Druid Priest and Priestesses. Somehow, we knew they were

there to speak to all mankind. But in the dreams, we heard no message. Each dream was similar, each time expecting to hear their voice and not being able to.

Once again, I couldn't tell you the message of the dream, but the feeling I was left with was one of awe mingled with presentiment and a tingling sense of awareness. I loved Rays, so I decided they were there to keep me company and lend their strength and beauty to my journey. Then the storm hit.

# Chapter 14–A Meeting with An Angry Mother Nature

I had just finished reefing down the stay sail again, dragging my body back to the cockpit. I felt like a helpless child, all hunched down, crawling on hands and knees. I tried to remember the storm Wayne and I had encountered and the exact moment I was finally able to realize how incredible it all was. I knew I had to get to that point soon or I would dissolve.

It started around 9:00 a.m. The morning before, after only three hours of sleep. A halyard wrapped itself around a protrusion on the mast and a frustrating hour was wasted just getting it clear. Then we were flying, Ko and me; not wanting to think about it then, yet knowing the winds were going to pick up. Sometimes you can just feel it in your bones, or in the uneven, gusty cough of the winds. Around 3:00 p.m. it began to howl; waves started building, whitecaps smashing, a bleak, menacing sky bullying everything around it until even the sun began to hide his wimpy little face. I inched forward and back so many times, reefing down the mainsail until it looked like a caricature of itself. Each time I stood to wrestle with the maniac lines, they fought like a prisoner, scrambling for release.

Each time I hooked myself on with 5-year-old safety gear, bracing against another clawing, grasping wave just so I could move forward and bring down the stay sail, my nerves tightened until my back, neck and shoulders felt as though they'd shrunk twenty times their size. Ko felt like a frightened animal, running wild through fire. I was running downwind, hoping it will eventually back down, but all I could see was a screaming, heaving ocean everywhere. Banshee winds. An enormous, angry energy raging into infinity and there was no one, nothing in sight except more and more of the same. The waves rose like some stone fist then smacked down so close to Ko I could feel her shudder.

I tried to hove-to, but the wheel stuck and I couldn't get Ko into the wind far enough to back the sail. Around and around I went until everything below deck lay withering, dying on the floorboards or plastered on the bulkheads. Nighttime dropped on top of us like a guillotine. Any chance of seeing a threatening trawler has just diminished by half. The minutes froze still, turning into hours, then weeks and I had never felt so alone in my life. A kind of desolate freezing rain, slamming saltwater waves, slap in your face all alone. I was afraid. I couldn't believe I was afraid. It's as simple as that. It was 10:00 p.m. Saturday night; a black, ugly, tormented night. A nightmare you can't awaken from. There's no safe harbor you can escape to. But it's the nightmare that forces you to put one step ahead of the other, do what has to be done. I went below, braced myself, thinking of Ko. I knew she was calling me to believe in the purpose of it all; believe that she's strong, capable and fearless. Belief and faith were all that was left in a stripped down, naked moment like that.

At about 1:00 p.m. Sunday afternoon it began calming down a little. The winds had pushed me off course. I knew I should do something about it but all I wanted to do was sit and take it all in. I made it. I went through my first storm, alone, at sea. My thoughts were so different than what I thought they'd be. It didn't feel like you imagined, like that picture of yourself as the heroine in some movie plot who can conquer all the travesties of nature, yelling to the world "we woman can do it too!" It felt deeper, quieter. A strange kind of pride, mixed with a fierce recognition you didn't really want to have–suddenly you get it–your pride and valor had to sit right next to your fear and loneliness. Side by side. They're sisters. One doesn't get to trump the other; they're equal partners. And this wild, screaming nature? I realized suddenly that I didn't want to 'conquer' anything at all, least of all this heaving ocean belly swollen with life.

Snuggling down behind the wheel grabbing hold of these thoughts, letting them swagger through my mind until they settle down, seemed like a good thing to do right then. Down thoughts! Down! The wind was completely still, I was physically and emotionally becalmed. Even the ocean swells seemed to be reacting in slow motion, heaving back and forth, gathering scattered bits and pieces of themselves that were tossed about by whatever just blew through. Everything felt turned all around, all sense of direction lost, squandered on rollicking waves and hyper thoughts. My compass, my GPS, both mechanically trained to point out reality could do nothing for that feeling that goes something like 'we-aint-you-aint-nobody aint-going-anywhere-today–you're grounded! Stranded like one tiny, solitary fish trapped in the middle of a circular 360-degree pond.

Even the sky and air around me was nothing! Just flat dull grays, turning into more flat dull grays. An empty horizon curves up, up and up, all around you, as though a clear translucent bowl has just been placed over all that exists. You know you've moved, the charts say so, but the keeper of the bowl never allows you to see any progress. All movement is an illusion. It's a strange feeling, one you want to hold on to–one you want to run away from. A perfectly balanced dance between waking and dreaming, emptiness and desire. You've been brought to a standstill, an impasse, a masterpiece of suspension; craving yet disdaining the hustle and bustle of activity; craving yet fearing the solitude and stillness. The need for both struggles then dissipates, even they can't hold their shape any longer. I could only think this must be what it feels like to be eyes wide open, wide awake inside the womb; because that's where I was. It felt dreamy, breathy, scattered with no need at all to care. Am I at the beginning? The end? Both? Or intriguingly enough, am I simply living a metaphor? Everything seems to be taking a pause for reflection, a pause centering around...what will you do with what you've learned today?

I can't help smiling at this, knowing I should be down on my knees giving thanks for being snatched from the jaws of death, from the jaws of this ruthless Mother Nature who cares not who she takes, but instead something else is going on. I am grateful! I am thankful! But not just for being spared my death. But because I've been handed another chance to re-think this idea of a ruthless, unfeeling Mother Nature. I believe I have just met the ultimate Crone. That wise woman we have turned into an ugly old witch, the one who gobbles up babies, mankind's testicles, and in her formless state gobbles up little sailboats like Ko.

She is ruthless! With an apparent lack of discrimination when it comes to life and death. But why do we feel so incensed about this? It came to me that if I could see death from her perspective, I might just begin to understand that death is also an exchange given, sooner or later, for the good of the whole; one more aspect of the service we give, of the balance and harmony that has always been Nature's legacy. Her same lack of discrimination is as apparent in her love, her nurture for the lives of every species, not just mankind. Is this not a perfect example of 'equality'? It would take a lot to live up to that sense of equality. What a strange twist of ego that Her sense of equality has been termed 'ruthless'.

So there you have it; just giving thanks for being snatched from the jaws of death suddenly didn't seem like enough. When I leave this womb, put my feet on land, will I fall back into all the pressures and fears that are so easy to succumb to? Will all these lessons just float away? Or will I remember how many chances we get to birth the visions we would have birthed had we remembered that we could? Will I remember the words of this Mother/Crone gave to me some time ago—in this world, all of us are in relationship to each other. Each of us hold some healing spark within our souls, some jewel to share with each other; the ways of mankind, the ways of creatures; the ways of the East and the West; the poets, the CEOs, the Pagans and the Christian. Each of us are capable of finding a way to serve and enhance the lives of all. I swore I would remember this, even knowing how likely I would forget.

A crazy pink-white seabird decided to move in with me. He or she landed on my cockpit combing, ass towards the galley entrance, dropping his stinky little waste petals all the way down the galley steps. He/she is so difficult to converse with. I shouted at him (deciding on a gender) to move his little tail feathers around, waved my arms and screamed, and all he did was look at me with those incredibly piercing eyes as if to say "Who do you think you are?" I don't know, I thought I was the captain of this boat.

"You little creep, you're shitting all over my galley!" Why is he not afraid of me? This makes no sense; I could have him for dinner.

"Dumb bird, dumb bird"

Two of his friends came to call, screeching overhead as if to say "She's a wild woman, come back to where it's safe!" Or maybe they're telling me that. I was confused. I was tired and evening was approaching. Or maybe the gray day just looked like that. I decided to sleep outside rather than the cabin below; me and my new feathered boyfriend. Fishing trawlers be damned; I hadn't slept in 24 hours or so.

I woke too soon to another squall that moved in to test Ko's strength and balance. All around me was a black night filled with creepy cloud formations; escapees from some cut-rate Hollywood movie set. I'd never hallucinated in my life, but I was pretty sure I was then, watching them drop out of the sky and step onto Ko's stern. I knew it wasn't real and wasn't mystical because I didn't like it. The seabird tucked its head under its wing and I thought 'perhaps I should do that too, but I'm not sure I'll fit. This is ridiculous, I'm going to have a chocolate chip cookie and just watch the show.' I loved chocolate chip cookies, they made it easy to think of wonderful, delicious thoughts. So I started thinking. Thinking of a world based on compassion, wisdom and vision. A world where children are safe to dream the impossible and old war vets are asked to share their sorrow, until their sorrow was just a memory of a time when we forgot to dream. A world in which earth speaks her power and vision of equality for all and history speaks that equality fell when the Earth fell into dominance and we fell out of balance, out of love. And we all remembered the time when we woke up and realized that peace was actually a functional way of life. I had to have another chocolate chip cookie on that one. Balance. Once again, the word became so much greater than it had ever been before. Why, how did we ever consent to giving over the enormous power of Spirituality to only one, cunning, jealous God alone; a God who warred and gobbled up every other God or Goddess around it. I instinctively knew then that we had a spiritual family, comprised of mother, father, grandmothers, siblings; that the mystery of Spirituality was way too enormous to be given over, totally, to one deity. It's funny what storms can teach you.

The false dawn was approaching. It didn't feel false to me. It felt like a child, leaping forth from the union of the receding night and the coming of the day and there is nothing more beautiful than to witness its birth. It makes you want to stick a flower behind your ear, dance under a full moon, hug the earth and all her inhabitants. It makes you want to stand up and say no to the destruction of beauty and Earth because you know that the destruction of both is the destruction of us. It's the in between times–night to day, day to night–and they are the most magical times of all, filled with that intense dawn-sapphire blue-silver color of energy filled with expectations and promises. Then suddenly the sun rises like a phoenix shot with fire into the sky. Hopefully, today will be filled with promise.

It was another cotton candy sky above. Everything seems to be in sync. I was sitting on the bow, tangerine in hand, juice dribbling down my cheek. It was just one of those days you know you're going to get company. Yep. A pod of pilot whales just wandered over to have a look-see.

Today's the day. I should be seeing Kosrae soon. It's taken me longer than expected, wandering all over this wet, slippery highway like some drunk drivin' sailor gal. But given the calms and squalls, I suppose there's some good reason why a seven-day journey turned into ten. And there is something on the horizon! It doesn't look like any ordinary cloud; seems stable, sold. I need to watch it, put the binoculars on it for a while before getting too excited. It's the nature of these gray snippy afternoons; very childish, love to play tricks on you. I have to turn away from it, leave it for an hour or so, then look again. When I do, I realize it's Kosrae! It has to be! She's here, just like a promise fulfilled, rising up from the aching, longing water like a mountainous temple; an elegant, lonely lady in a vast, vast water-land. Beckoning with safe anchorage, adventure and undiscovered treasures. All that's left to do is just watch and gaze at her like some puppy dog, watching its mistress' shadow loom up ahead. If had a tail,

I'd be wagging! Is this what those ancient navigators felt? A precious, burning ember moment that has remained the same throughout all time? And like some green sea fraternity, that same urge to scream–land ho! Blow the conch!–break out the rum, the harmonica, the revelry–blessed be, we made it!–can be heard like echoes from an ocean time chamber. A tiny beacon of land is sighted, a speck of paint surreptitiously dropped on the canvas of an empty horizon; a focal point for the eye of a weary traveler.

There's no way I'll make it today and that's OK., there's lots to do. A gal has to be presentable when she pulls into port. The only clothes I've worn out here is a lava-lava and a t-shirt who's smell reminds me I need something more than a salt water submersion. Ko too! She looked a mess and still had an oil mustache on her hull from Tarawa. But we'll take care of that later, right now it's a good time for a toast to what will be my last night alone at sea.

Watching the sun set, taking Kosrae with it, leaving those murky blue-black shadows in its wake, makes me wonder if she'll appear again tomorrow. This Sleeping Lady; will she be watching my arrival at her feet? Who are her people, her children? What songs, chants, dances has she inspired? I couldn't wait to find out.

For most of the evening I watched for any fishing boats and dozed off when I felt safe enough to do so. The night stretched on beyond its limits, it seemed. But I didn't mind, knowing I was going in to harbor tomorrow sometime. I woke the next morning, at dawn, watching the last star sentries give way to a beautiful boasting sunrise of deep rose, purples and whatever other colors there's no name for. It was perfect, and filled me with passion and energy.

# Chapter 15—Micronesia

I circled half way around the island until I was pretty sure I'd spotted the Lelu harbor entrance, ditched my sails, turned on the engine and suddenly I had company.

"Calling the sail boat Ko Lea, this is the 'island boy' fishing boat on your port side, come in."

"Yes, come in island boy, this is Ko Lea. What can I do for you?" It wasn't your regulation style call numbers, but I figured it would do.

"Do you want an escort into the harbor? There are some ugly reefs going in."

"I'm all yours!" I called back.

As we entered, I looked up and saw the mountain formation that made up 'The Sleeping Lady' and knew I was safe for the time I'd be here. The formation showed a woman laying on her back with her long green tresses flowing down the mountain side. And I was going to anchor under her wing for a while.

The two ex-pats from 'Island Boy' led me to a safe place to anchor, then gave me some much-needed information on where to find Customs and Immigration tomorrow. I would have to go to them, but I was certainly ready. I spotted my New Zealand friends from Friendship while coming in. I knew they'd beat me here; it was an amazingly fast and quite 'techy' yacht.

I had 2 bottles of wine for my first night at harbor and it was close to 5:00 when I finally cleaned Ko up enough to relax and button down for the evening. Definitely wine time. I just wanted to watch the sunset, have a little wine and stretch my legs out on the cockpit. You can't imagine what it feels like to know that you will sleep the whole night through with no thought to an oncoming trawler or ocean monster at your heels. I could have cried.

I was below deck preparing a cheese quesadilla when I heard...

"Permission to come aboard."

It was Toni, from Guatemala. She and her husband had sailed into Kosrae a couple of months ago on board their trimaran "Indigo". "I heard there was a single-handed sailor gal coming in and I wondered if it was you. How the hell are ya doing?"

You'll have to settle for red wine, it's all I have, so get on up here and have a glass" I replied, realizing that my first night at anchor was not going to be the quiet evening I was hoping for. But Toni had stories. A million of them. And I was in for quite a few laughs and knew I'd enjoy it. She and her husband actually had sailed around the world, maybe even twice. Her skills were so far above my own it was pitiful!

She filled me in as much as she could on Kosrae; it was very religious, closed down completely on Sundays; there were ancient ruins right in the middle of town made from a certain kind of rock found only on the furthest side of the mountains, the Micronesians believed they were 'whistled or sang' from the other side; the monsoons were almost unbearable and you'll probably die from old age before they stop; you could hitch hike all over the island with no trouble at all; but then you could take your dingy through all the waterways all over the island as well; not much night life but hiking through the mountains was a religious experience.

"When you want to go into town, just dingy over to Raza's land" she pointed at a little palapa house to my left you could barely see in the dark haze of night. "He'll drive you crazy with stories about his ancestors, but he's nice enough."

"You'll love this Kathleen, apparently their Breadfruit Goddess appeared to the early islanders and told them to leave because a great death was coming. Supposedly that's why the island's population was so sparse when the first explorers came."

She knew I'd love it because Toni wasn't much on islanders, "the old ways", and their way of life or their Gods and Goddesses. But in fact, a plague did hit these islands not long after many islanders had left. We had a lot of discussions about it in Guatemala, disagreeing about many things but I loved her exuberance for throwing around her opinions. She was one of those people who got you excited about getting into an argument. I really loved her, despite our differences.

The next day I hitchhiked to Immigrations and Customs. Got a ride from a very generous man who took me to meet his family and share their lunch. He shared many stories of when Micronesia was owned by the Japanese, then by the United states after the war via a boon from the pope at that time. I don't know about you, but it seems to me a little strange that these tiny little nations can just be handed over as a war prize to some other country. Several years prior to my arrival however, Micronesia received its own sovereignty from the U.S., although it is still under the thumb of the U.S. through the Compact Agreement. I was to find out more of that during my time in Pohnpei.

I finally got back to Raza's house around 3:00 and he immediately took me for a tour of his ancestors' pictures, most of whom had been the local chiefs. I was quite fascinated by it all. He showed me a copy of a Captain's log, one of the 1st vessels to ever reach the island. I opened it and was totally blown away when I read the Captain's last name, Christian. I immediately wondered if he was an ancestor of Fletcher Christian of The Bounty. Raza told me to take it and read it if I wanted to. Did I want to? Ah, Yeah! I rowed back to Ko and prepared to settle down for some heavy reading.

I never found out if these two Christians were related but I did find out some interesting details about his records of the island's history. He took it upon himself to correct the islander's confusion about God, completely deleting all reference to any feminine Deity. He made no mention of a Breadfruit Goddess. I found myself quite angry at the arrogance of this man. How many details of the lives of the indigenous around the world have been portrayed incorrectly due to the haughtiness of such a man?

I rowed over to Fellowship the following day for an early afternoon tea. Millie was such a good cook!

"Have you seen the ruins yet?" I asked.

"Oh yes; the kids were extremely under impressed! It's actually hard to see them, they're so covered over with growth, vines, and the like. I hear the ones in Pohnapei, however, are quite huge and well taken care of.

"Toni was telling me that the locals believed they were sung, or whistled from one side of the island to the other. Have you heard that as well?"

"Quite. No one knows how they got where they are. Realistically, there was no way they could have been moved at that time. They are ancient." She poured me another glass of wine then continued. "However, I do remember reading that Einstein believed there was a sound that, when uttered correctly, could actually move matter from one place to the other. I have to believe he wasn't jesting"

"I love the mysteries, the inexpiable plopped into our laps just to scramble our little egos!"

We all hung around Kosrae so we could experience Thanksgiving in the village church. It was an amazing day full of generosity and happiness. People from all over Kosrae, not just Lelu, came to the service and in the middle of it, each village marched in and began tossing out gifts to everyone who attended. The little bag I caught had a pair of hand-made kitchen towels, shells, and trinkets. Afterwards we went outside to a feast that lasted for hours. The generosity of the Kosraeans was truly awe-inspiring.

There were no homeless, no hungry in Micronesia. All the land belongs to them, and everyone had a plot for themselves given by the Chief of whatever county they lived in; or at least that was how it was when I was there. Breadfruit, banana trees, all sorts of fruit trees were shamelessly abundant, and fishing for supper was a family thing. It was a living lesson on how capitalism actually contributes to poverty.

It was time to leave for all of us however. Millie, Steve and the kids were off to Palau, Toni and Jerome were off to Borneo, and Ko and I decided to make a run for it to Pohnpei, which was the capital of Micronesia. I had $50 left and couldn't begin to tell you how nervous I was about that. I wasn't sure what I'd find in Pohnpei, if anything at all. But just maybe there would be some job I could pick up.

The sail over was quite raucous. The winds were tossing clouds around the sky, then all of a sudden, they'd stop all together, leaving us in a slump with floppy sails. Ko was probably dreaming again of that good steady wind she always moans and groans about when she's stumbling around in this slop and chop. But eventually we sighted land and headed into the main harbor of Pohnpei. I tied up to the docks among a plethora of fishing trawlers, and awaited Customs and Immigration. I met another sailor who was also waiting and the following day we both dropped anchor next to Sokhes Island in the turquoise water of a horseshoe harbor surrounded by mangroves, palm trees and verdant green mountains. There was a little bar right next to the dingy dock that everyone frequented in the evenings, including my own first night there.

Pohnpei was so different from Kosrae; haughty and lush! Sophisticated and petulant.

And it smelled like the color of green, spiced with oranges and lemongrass. I immediately knew I was going to love it.

It was at that same little bar that I met Jenny; an American lawyer working at the Federated States of Micronesia Congress.

"Are you serious? You're actually looking for a job? Oh, Lady, do I have a perfect job for you!" she smiled like a Cheshire cat; It made me wonder exactly what she had in mind.

"You're either my new best friend, or a trickster. I'll bite. What do you have in mind?"

"Well, I work for Congress and we desperately need another proofreader for next Session. Can you do that?"

"Oh yeah, definitely. Read the sentence backwards, all the tricks." Boy was I excited.

"O.K., come over tomorrow around 11:00 and meet with Dennis, our administrator. Can't promise, but I'm sure he'll hire you." And there it was. My miracle. I was hired for a whopping $5.00 an hour, but it was $5.00 an hour more than I've had in a long long time!

It was there, at the Congress that I met Alysa. My boss. A young woman who was half Micronesian and half American, educated in the States and one of the most beautiful women I've ever met. Alabaster skin with freckles, black curly hair that framed her heart shaped face. But most of all, it was her attitude of immense intelligence, humor and grace that struck me as memorable. At that time, she had 2 children, one of which was a babe in her arms. She had just given birth about 2 months before. And that led me to one of the most intriguing experiences I'd had up to that time. There she sat in her office, babe at her bare breast, nursing, while checking files on the computer when Dennis walked me in to be introduced. And there she sat bare breasted, feeding her young one, anytime one of the Senators came in, the President, other secretaries, lawyers; all the while with the composure of a dignified CEO. I was going to love working here. And even more so when I learned that so many of the Senators wore their skirt-like lava-lavas and festive shirts to session rather than suits and ties.

We had so much in common, Alysa and I. We talked of natural healing and natural childbirth; she had given birth alone each time. We shared our mystical experiences and dreams; she told me about the time she had given birth to All-Miya, her first child (she had named her that to express that she was all hers). She was living alone in a small hut and worried constantly about scorpions biting All-Miya. One night she dreamed of this plant high in the mountains that would heal any scorpion bite. When she went to find it, it was exactly where it was pictured in her dream. She told me about living with her mom most of her life in the States. She had a chance to marry a fairly well-to-do lawyer.

"I knew in my heart, though, that I'd have to give up my Micronesian ways if I did. I thought about it for a long long time, and realized I just couldn't do it." she said.

"So you hightailed it back here to live instead?" I asked.

"Yeah, it broke my mother's heart, but I knew it would be better for me. And All-Miya, she was his daughter."

"Do you ever miss the opulence, or opportunities you'd have had living in the states?" I understood what she was saying, but still I wondered.

"No; I don't think so at least. Do you ever wonder if most people really stop and think about the kind of values they want to live by? Peace vs. success; hustle and stress rather than living your own pace? Or, just being able to be exactly who you are with no silent inquiry? These were the questions my mom and I bantered about before I left."

I felt that sitting before me was someone who really did know herself, her faults, fears and desires. I was proud to call her a friend.

Pohnpei gave me so many wonders and so many lessons:

- Drinking Kava Kava at some local bar with the president, or senators, with no secret service men around. They just simply had no fear of their people.

- The rigmarole of getting into the US embassy, searching of the car, searching you, going through boarded up windows and doors, vs. the open-door embassy of Australia, even while they were out to lunch, you could just go on in and use the computers.

- Reading the Jesuit logs of the beliefs of the islanders; finding out that they their version of the great flood was far different than most people's versions contrary to so many claims that the story is the same all over earth; the Great Mother found out how abusive they were to Her Daughter, Earth, gave them warning, but when unheeded, unleashed the great flood.

- Discovering that the much maligned view point of banning certain foods by the chiefs was not due to their greed, but due to seasonal wisdom; don't eat this fruit during the cold season, the red banana must be protected for mothers who are nursing, oysters, shell fish should not be eaten during certain times of the year, this fruit sustains you during summer. There was a lot of animosity between the US States' control and the control of the local chiefs.

· Finding out the red banana had more nutrition than any baby food imported to Micronesia. This especially was a major concern of mine—commercial, imported foods—how could we publicize the benefits of something so abusive just for the sake of commerce?

I spent 4 years in Pohnpei finding out more and more about the control the US had with the Compact Agreement. Just before I left, the US was advocating the sale of property to Japanese interest, who wanted to secure an investment in Micronesia; luxury hotels, private condos. And with it all, Micronesia would have to join the World Bank, and promise to set a limit on wages; no local could make more than $7 an hour. It was time for me to leave, I couldn't control the outrage I was feeling while proofreading the text of the bills that may put all of this into effect. I'm not a very good employee.

I do know this, that despite Micronesia becoming a country with the highest percentage of diabetes, due to imported canned foods, sugar, and loss of their indigenous ways; they campaign heavily towards breast feeding, reinstating the red banana once again reviving their ancient ways. I have to believe that Alysa has a hand in this.

Nan Madol, the center of the mysterious ruins in Micronesia, was as mystifying as any ancient ruins around the world. It is said the building of Nan Madol began as early as 900 AD, but some say much earlier. The history beginning with the mysterious brothers Olsihpa and Olsohpa, believed to have been the Sorcerers who sang the stones across the island to build Nan Madol. Some say they were tyrants who ruled the islands, others say they benevolent rulers who brought the islands together under one rule. I only knew the ruins to be as beautiful as any you could imagine, with the man-made canals, basalt stone walls, over grown with vines and bright white/purple orchids and the tingle of magic. Stepping upon the ruins you got the sense of walking through a grave yard with the ghosts of the past brushing up against your skin. When I visited, I always brought sage, tobacco and flowers. It gave me a feeling of belonging somehow, a feeling of family.

Part of Nan Madol lay beneath the ocean; just outside the harbor was a public beach and snorkel place. On the floor of the ocean, you could see stone steps that formed a path leading from the beach. You could follow them for quite a ways until the ocean floor dropped off to never-never land. I wasn't a diver, so never got to follow it all the way out. Pohnpei translates to "upon the altar" and Nan Madol translates to "the space between". It was a definite nod to the magic of the tiny island, and the ruins; 'the space between' relates to the ether space, in between realities, the magic spaces. It was an easy domain to fall in love with!

# Chapter 16–Parting with Ko'Lea

I began to feel my time in Micronesia was coming to an end; I could recognize the signs. I began to feel restless, and antsy; I was becoming sloppy, getting into arguments with the lawyers about the upcoming bills; heated discussions about women's rights with the local Jesuit Priest; and quite a few other snippets along the way. My dad was very ill, and I really needed to return home. I wanted another chance to beat him in cards. What plagued me the most was knowing that my time as a single-handed sailor had also come to an end. I needed to say good-bye to Ko. A very dear friend who also was a lawyer for one of the main courts had always loved Ko as much as I. I contacted him to see if he still interested in purchasing her.

"I'll have the money for you in the next couple of days," was his answer. I could almost hear him yelling 'Yippee,' except that wasn't very lawyer like.

My last night aboard Ko was spent gazing up at Sokhes Island, under a radiant full moon, with a slight breeze rocking us ever so gently. I knew it was going to be almost impossible to leave her. I did what I always did when I felt cocooned in her arms. I brought a bottle of wine and a glass up to the bow, and leaning against the combing, I started to talk to her. Because that's what sailors do, they talk to their boats when their hearts are sorrowful.

"Ko, remember that 1st crazy sail to Lanai we had? Trying to let the sail out and I was pulling on the wrong line?"

"Yeah" she said, "You had me stumbling all over those waters before we got it straight."

I could always hear Ko in my head when we talked, she really was like a sister.

"And the phosphorescence in that little horseshoe harbor we anchored in when you dared me to jump in and swim through it?"

Her head dipped a little, like she was thinking. "I loved that harbor; one of my most favorite of all! Oh, and do you remember that young kid who sneaked on board in the middle of the night? I think he said he loved you."

"Oh My Goddess! I do!" I slammed my palm into my forehead.

"You handled it so well, Kat; telling him to go wait up on my cockpit while you got up"

Kat was what she called me. And I remembered that story all too well. It took me nearly 2 glasses of wine each to convince him to jump back overboard and swim to shore.

"So many stories, Ko. So many stories we have between us. How can I share them all?"

I looked out over the tiny anchorage, watching the moon light up its path on the water, watching the colors shift, growing and receding, and I couldn't help but feeling I was in Paradise.

Paradise. I had always felt Earth was, and is, the original Eden. Paradise. It was just our inability to see 'what is' that kept us from knowing it. I started to drift into that thought and began thinking of Eve. Garden Eve. Lady Eve. Mother, daughter, slut with the power to drive men from their chaste morality, saddle women with an irreparable reputation; she who makes apple cheeked priests blush, yet also makes it possible for the merchants of strung beads, statues that bleed, Vaticans and chapels to become wealthy, healthy and wise.

OK, so right on. Who was she, or, what was she? A woman who could hear, but feared the voice of nature? A woman who heard the call of transformation but could or would not heed the summons? Did she, through her fears, bring on the power of patriarchy? The power of war? Or was she simply a metaphor of a power men feared. The only thing I knew for sure was she's a sister. She's was part of our Tribe. And I needed to find out the truth. So, naturally, I asked Ko.

"What fell?" she queried as she gracefully turned with the current, now facing the mangroves. "Think like a woman. Use your gut instincts, look at the story as though a woman were creating it. What's your story?"

I hate riddles. What fell? A century long power struggle ensues to break the hold of the matriarchs, spiritually and politically. A group of monks write a book to condone their power struggle. Given the situation, just like their use of the Pagan Holidays, they would have had to use a familiar legend, a beloved story, twisted just enough to instill fear, doubt and finally lead to absolute control.

"Oh my bloody heart, I got it, Ko. We've been looking at that story strictly through the eyes of men, upside down, with blinders on."

"Ummm, wasn't that exactly what I just said?" Ko was a last word freak.

"Stories. They change, or get twisted depending on the agenda of those telling them. So, let's imagine the original."

Taking a sip of wine, I started to think like the Matriarchs of old. What story would they need to tell their daughters? What piece of wisdom or advice would they need to pass on? I closed my eyes, asked my Guide to bring me some insight and this is what came:

Once there lived a young maiden who was coming of age. Born at sunset she was called Eve and grew into a beautiful, long legged young girl; happy and vital. As her body began to change into a woman, so too did her senses. Colors became more brilliant; sounds became more distinct. Her awareness increased three-fold–that of her environment, all the creatures that lived with her, and the people of her Tribe. She became so in tune with all that was around her that she had no fear. With her new-found communion with all life, she realized that she could converse with the creatures, and plant life, simply by being still enough to listen; with her heart, her senses and her intuition. They taught her many things, the union of all life, giving back to one another, and the great circle of life that sustained all within it; this was, they taught, what prosperity, abundance and greatness truly is. By eating the grapes, the berries, the roots and the fruit of the trees she would learn their needs, receive their wisdom, know their knowledge. Each creature taught her skills; the stealth of the leopardess, grace of the fawn, eternal curiosity and joy of the monkey and strength of the bear. But what she loved the most was the transformation and regeneration of Snake. She understood there was promise in transformation, evolution and eternal hope, so Snake became her greatest mentor. With the help of them all, she understood her role in keeping the balance within all life. She was opening up to her greater self.

But she was young, and in love. She wanted nothing more than to share all the wonder and joy with her mate. The elder mothers warned her 'this is the legacy of the great mystery' they said, 'do not share your medicine with those who are unable to accept it' they said. But she could not anticipate the anger, loathing and desire for control it would bring from those who could not feel the purpose behind this great legacy. And so she tried to share, and instead of joy, found contempt, condemnation, separation, ridicule, judgment and subjugation. So Eve closed off her senses, her intuition; turned a blind eye to what she knew, what she felt; but most horrific of all, she silenced her voice. A great darkness then fell upon the world, the creatures wept for they could no longer hear her speak; fear, suspicion and separation coursed through the lands and Our Mother Earth shook violently at the loss of her daughter's touch. Balance had been lost to the world.'

For me it was an insight which had summed up the years of questions I'd had since the beginning of my journey; we've been carrying the burden of Eve on our shoulders, the burden of a story about Women, by allowing it's interpretation to come from men; most particularly from men devoted to stamping out the matriarchal way of life and all those who wished to honor it. The ramifications of that are staggering.

The parable of Eve was a warning, but not the warning we have been led to believe. It was a warning that had been completely twisted, and manipulated to perpetrate an agenda of absolute control. I was angry, but at the same time, relieved.

However, I wish I could verify Eve's story, as given to me in meditation, as truth. I cannot. Yet everything inside me, my body, mind and soul, tells me that there is truth within it, even if only in its intention. I could never understand the reason behind the biblical story of Eve–punishment of an entire gender for centuries for the failure of obedience to a jealous tyrannical God? For what possible purpose except absolute control over this gender.

I thought about the centuries of women's subjugation and oppression; the centuries of our wisdom and inherent knowledge lost to patriarchal control. About the economic and social distortion that has come about with the loss of our voice, our inherent knowledge, our intuitive understanding of the great circle of life. I thought about the generations of women who passed on the subjugation to their daughters compounding that imbalance for centuries.

Had the old wise Matriarchs continued to exert their power, they would have balked at and fought every transgression against Earth, and all its species. We would have had generations of women standing boldly, aggressively addressing early American politics; women who were heard and listened to as they spoke out against slavery, the loss of indigenous wisdom and culture, women who demanded balance between technology and humanity. If they were in government today, it is possible we would have quite a dissimilar society; we would have a path to balance, to compassion, to an educational system rooted in a holistic ideology; we would have had a chance to bring about peace. A dream? Maybe. But I'd like to think of it as a vision. A vision of what could have been, yet what is more important, what is still possible. Can we repair it?

We can repair it! We simply have to remember who we are. We are not, we were never meant to simply be "equal to men". We were meant to be equal to Women...the Wise Women of knowledge who will speak, act and stand up in their own image and likeness. We were always meant to be equal only to the great legacy we are.

If an ability, a heritage, a voice or gift is oppressed long enough; if it is shut down and devalued generation after generation, it will eventually be thought of only as an old wife's tale, a myth, or a fairy tale, with very little to do with reality now. And that is what has happened. But my heart and soul (and indeed, my entire journey) tells me that our gifts and abilities are not completely lost; that they never could be as long as Mother Earth is still alive. Do all women have mystical abilities? I think we do, always have had. We simply need to believe in ourselves and reacquaint ourselves with our legacy. Do men also have our instincts? Yes, certainly, but only if they are deeply connected to their own Feminine side.

Now you have read my story and my journey, and my commitment to you is the truth of everything I have told you. I pass this on to whoever will listen with hope and love in my heart. Do with it what you wish, but if it stirs even the slightest flicker of truth within, I ask that you think long and hard, then let the possibility of that truth enter your heart. We have never been abandoned by the Great Mother, and never will we be! But so far, we have been unable to stem the tide of rape and destruction of Mother Earth, her children and all species. I believe we all know that it is time to be seen, to be heard; It's time to stand up in our own image and likeness, and become known as Women of Power; time to re-forge our ancient link with the Goddess and Mother Earth. Let's re-join our sisterhood and once again become a Tribe.

# The Guide Speaks

You are Woman! You are Mother Earth's Daughters.
Together, we are A Tribe of Women; the keepers of wisdom
and balance between all the Elements and Dimensions that
live on and within our Earth Mother. You have been given gifts
on so many levels, in so many dimensions. And yet I hear so
many of you wail about the need to be equal to men. Why?
Why do you put men on such a pedestal? Why are they the
criteria of what is to be honored? It can only be because you
do not know of, nor believe in, your own heritage. The powers
you hold that are so far above that criteria. I light my cheroot
and smile; I see a time when men will desire to become equal
to women. But not until you begin to own your power. Do you
remember listening to the roar of the ocean and heard Her
calling you? Or as a child, how you had an uncanny affinity for
healing herbs, and the ability to sense the nature of plants
and knew you had to do something with that affinity? Do you
remember the dreams you had that came true? Or were
compelled to speak the truth, despite your fear? And at the
same time, you instinctively knew each time you were being
lied to. Do you still cry, brokenhearted over injustice when you
see it, and wish there was something you could do? Or all the
times your skin prickled and knew you were being warned?
Remember sneaking all those books on magic into your room,
pouring over them, feeling like you'd come home? These were
all times you were being asked to remember how huge you
are! Your greater self always sees the potential you carry,

always sending you signs of your gifts and talents. You are woman⋯your greatest spiritual teachings are held within Mother Earth, given at her bosom, nurtured with absolute love; then inspired through instinct, affinity and impulse. The spiritual essence that is of the Feminine is as active and free flowing as Mother Ocean. It is a living breathing essence, and contains a living breathing language. Can you contain it within the rules and dogma of those who do not understand it? Who do not wish to honor it? Those who crave dogma seldom tolerate such spiritual essence. If you must speak softly, then learn to do so with the force of an earth quake. For that is the force of Wisdom behind you. This is your legacy! Bring Vision back to your soul, for Vision is also one of your greatest gifts. Heed them well, nourish it all and you will nourish all life. Remember, it is here, at this fragile point of choice, that one takes a giant leap forward, creating space for a larger you to appear. Leap, my sisters! She's waiting for you.

# Chapter 17–One More Story, Bali, Indonesia; the Beginning of a New Life

Just before I had sold my cafe, I had a dream. Another one of those you know as prophetic, a message, a calling to you from something greater.

In my dream I was living in a desert, perhaps Iranian, could have been Egypt. I had a very luxurious tent with soft oriental rugs inside and colorful embroidered pillows scattered everywhere. I was outside when I saw a mother elephant walk over to me with her babe. She went into my tent and I of course followed. I was quite curious about why she was there. She sat down and faced me, put her feet up and beckoned me to rub them. I spent about an hour doing so while she talked and talked, telling me her woes, her griefs and her joys. Although I could not remember a thing she said, I understood she was sharing her life with me. And I was very happy to accommodate her while her babe played at my side.

When I awoke, I knew it was a message but I figured it must have something to do with body work and I really disliked doing massage work on others. I was just simply not going to be a masseuse. So I stored the dream in my heart and waited to get more clarity on it.

When I left Micronesia I decided to go to Bali and spend at least 2 months there before going home. And there, in Bali, I finally received the clarity I wanted from that long-ago dream. Bali–I just stepped into yet another living example of paradise. That Bali was exceptionally beautiful was not the only notable thing about the experience; it was her people. They perpetuated the beauty with sheer intention and focus. Everything they did imbued beauty; from the statues they erected at the entrance to each village, to the flowers and incense they placed outside the entrance to their shops, to the temples they worshiped in, even in the clothes they wore to worship, chant, and dance. The incredible grace and talent of the Balinese dancers was thrilling, but it was the 21 separate eye movements they had to learn before they could perform that stunned me. The Balinese were animist. Which means aside from their Gods and Goddesses, they also had animal Deities. One of which was Ganesh, the elephant God of prosperity and joy. It was here that I was introduced to Ganesh and his Mother, whom some say are the same. I was infatuated with them. I had always been infatuated with elephants!

Not long after our introduction I saw a sign advertising Reflexology lessons. I immediately went back to my dream; without a doubt I understood the message. Ganesh, Mother Ganesha had been calling me to become a Reflexologist. Call it what you like, but I knew I would be great at it! So there, in Bali, Indonesia, I set about to begin the next chapter in my life. Soon after, I flew home and set up practice in a tiny little town called Sedro Woolley, Washington. I spent 18 years building my practice and opening a small but effective metaphysical healing center.

Now I am on another journey. Rather than a sailboat, I've chosen a land cruiser-a small motor home for me and my dog Raika. We are happy wanderers on Mother Earth, once again spending each day in a new place of wonder and beauty!

~~~~ ~~~~

Made in the USA
Monee, IL
14 July 2020